Dentists, Social Workers, Skilled Trades, Lawyers, Nurses, Psychologists, and Writers

Short and Simple Explanation Series - 7 Books in 1

Louis Bevoc

Published by
NutriNiche System LLC

Louis Bevoc books...simple explanations of complex subjects

Dentists

Short and Simple Explanation Series
Book 1

Louis Bevoc

Published by
NutriNiche System LLC

Louis Bevoc books...simple explanations of complex subjects

Introduction

Introduction

This is the first book in a series of short and simple explanations of professions. For every book, the profession is described along with a discussion on the required education and training. These books are written so people can inform and educate themselves on various professions without having to understand difficult language or complex terminology...which is the underlying philosophy of all Louis Bevoc books.

Unbeknownst to some people, dentistry is a branch of medicine. Practicing dentists typically diagnose and treat diseases in the oral cavity of the face where humans eat, drink, breath, and make vocal sounds...commonly known as the mouth. Another aspect of dentistry that is not well-known is the fact that dentists work on more than teeth. Their work deals with people's jaws, sinuses, roots, tongues, throats, ears, and other areas of the face including the head and temples. They do not perform work on ears, heads, and temples, but they need to understand how these areas affect the mouth. For example, some people get headaches or earaches when they have problems with their teeth or after those teeth are repaired.

Dentists also need to understand bone structure. They sometimes need to strengthen or rebuild bone in their patients in order to perform the necessary dental work, so understanding the strength and density of those bones is important. This is why the study of anatomy is an important aspect of a dentist's formal education.

Finally, dentists need to know to know if their patients have allergies to drugs and medications so they know which ones should be avoided. Along the same lines, they need to understand their patients' allergic reactions to the material and equipment used. For example, some people are allergic to latex so latex gloves cannot be used during any dental procedure.

Some dental procedures can be handled by one dentist, while other procedures require a team of people. Typically team consists of assistants or hygienists, but a specialist might also be on hand for specific problems that arise. The procedures are usually conducted in a private business owned by the practicing dentist or a group of partners. However, the dental work can be done in other institutions such as hospitals, correctional facilities, and military bases. Regardless of where the procedures are performed, the goal is to help people with tooth and gum related health issues while making them as comfortable as possible.

Dentists cannot perform every type of dental work available because the training and education required are far too excessive for them to complete and comprehend. The profession needs to be subdivided to provide patients with individual expertise so, similar to medical doctors, it is broken down into sub-categories for specialization purposes. These sub-categories assure patients that they will get the best care possible from competent and well-trained dentists.

Now you have been introduced to the branch of medicine known as dentistry, so let's move forward into more detailed discussions of the profession. The next section discusses specific types of dentists who practice all over the world.

Types

As mentioned earlier, dentists cannot perform every procedure in their profession. They are not familiar with some problems that arise, so they consult the help of dental specialists with detailed trading in the designated problem areas.   These specialists focus on different aspects of dentistry such as tooth replacement, bone structure, and gum disease. They are typically referred by general dentists after those general dentists discover issues outside of their personal expertise.

The dental profession is often broken down into specialist categories that include those listed below. Please note that, in reality, dental education and training are long and arduous processes; thereby making the descriptions below unjustified in terms of complexity and difficulty. However, this book is designed to provide short and simple explanations of dentists' jobs, so these descriptions are appropriate for relaying the necessary information.

General dentist

Description

These professionals make up the most well known type of dentists. Often referred to as the primary care dentist, these professionals are typically the first stop for tooth related issues, and they recommend treatment to other dentists when they believe the skills of a specialist are necessary.

General dentists are capable of performing a variety of different services for their patients including cleanings, X-rays, exams, cavity fillings, tooth extractions, bridges, crowns, and root canals. However, the scope of these professionals' work to limited to basic dental care procedures. When the work is complex, general dentists recommend specialized care from dentists who have intensive training in the areas where the problems exist. This does not mean that general dentists cannot perform the required work; it simply means that they want to refer that work to someone who is better qualified.

Education and training

The majority of general dentists complete an undergraduate degree before entering dental school. There is technically no official "pre-dental" program, but typically the degree is science-based with chemistry and microbiology in the curriculum.

Dental school programs are accredited by the American Dental Association (ADA) and take about four years to complete. This coursework is designed to educate students and expose them to the various aspects of the general dental profession. While earning this doctoral degree, aspiring dentists often perform work on cadavers or human volunteers for real-world experience purposes.

At the completion of dental school, general dentists are usually required to undergo a residency for several years where they have access to mentors and situations requiring their newfound expertise. Once this residency is completed, these individuals must take and pass an examination administered by The American Board of General Dentistry, and then they are able to obtain a license and begin their practice.

Pediatric dentist

Description

A simple explanation of a pediatric dentist is a dentist who performs dental work on children beginning with the presence of their first tooth (or teeth) and ending when they reach adolescence. Since children mature at different ages, some kids remain under pediatric dental care longer than others. In short, there is no age where children automatically move into being a patient of an adult dentist (typically a general dentist).

Pediatric dentists' main function is to detect early tooth decay and put preventative measures into effect before that decay leads to more serious problems. Most of these preventative measures are geared toward educating parents because the parents need to take action by properly instructing their children on what they need to do. Sometimes these measures involve basic disease prevention care such as flossing and brushing, but they can also be designed to prevent injury or damage to teeth and gums. For example, children who suck their thumb for long periods of time could push teeth out of place as they grow through the gums. Additionally, children who put objects into their mouths risk injuring their gums. Stopping kids from putting objects in their mouth might seem easy because it is basic common sense, but some children want to taste everything they pick up so constant monitoring of their behavior is necessary.

Education and training

Pediatric dentists differ from general dentists who work on children's' teeth because they must undergo more education and training before they can obtain a license to practice. In short, pediatric dentists are trained specifically on children's dental care while most other dentists' training is geared toward adults.

These professionals must first earn their science-based undergraduate degrees and then enter dental school. Once in dental school, they need to earn a doctoral degree. During the process and after the completion of this degree, they go through training. However, they must complete a pediatric dental residency program before they can become certified to practice.

The pediatric dental residency program starts after students graduate from dental school and it lasts approximately two years. This program consists of clinical work and scientific study under an experienced mentor, and it differentiates itself from other dental residencies because child psychology, child pharmacology, child development, and child surgery are the main focus. Children are treated as patients with special needs because they cannot be subjected to certain types of treatment given to adults such as anesthesia procedures.

After the pediatric residency is completed, the aspiring pediatric dentist must study for and pass both parts of the National Board Dental Examination in order to be licensed to practice. This exam includes standardized testing to evaluate the preparedness of these individuals to open a practice for the dental care of children. Specific countries, states, or regions might require additional testing, but, for the most part, these dental graduates are now considered pediatric dentists.

Periodontist

Description

These dentists diagnose and treat diseases of the soft tissue surrounding teeth (typically the gums), and one of the most well-known diseases they treat is gingivitis. Gingivitis causes the gums to become swollen and bleed and, if left untreated, can turn into a more serious disease known and periodontitis (periodontal disease). When periodontitis takes over, the gums begin to pull away from the teeth; thereby producing gaps and exposing portions of the teeth that are not normally showing under healthy conditions. This disease is serious because bone structure can deteriorate as bone is lost and teeth might fall out with little or no prompting.

Periodontists are becoming more and more common for deep cleanings of teeth that extend down underneath the gums. Once thought of as unnecessary, people are changing their opinions about these practitioners and starting to frequent their services. This change in attitude is partially due to suggestions (or pressure) from general dentists, but the point is that periodontists are becoming increasingly popular.

Essentially, the work of periodontists involves a diagnosis of the gum tissue using a probe for surface analysis and x-rays for a more detailed view. Millions of people are affected by some type of gum disease, and older adults are classified as the highest risk category. Gum disease can be prevented with proper oral hygiene because it is typically due to a bacteriological buildup, but, unfortunately, many people do not take the necessary preventative measures and end up needing the services of a Periodontist.

Education and training

After earning a science-based undergraduate degree, aspiring periodontists need to enter and complete dental school. However, dental school graduation is not the end of the road for these individuals. Before they can practice, they need to have training specific to their field under an experienced mentor. This training typically takes three years because there is a lot of detailed information to absorb and understand. After their training, aspiring periodontists need to take an exam administered by The American Board of Periodontology. Once the exam has been passed, periodontists become licensed and can begin to practice.

Prosthodontist

Description

Although not necessarily a household name, prosthodontists are a specialized category of dentistry that perform needed services for many people. These dentists are very knowledgeable about dental implants, bridges, crowns, and dentures. Their services are sometimes not covered by dental insurance programs because they are considered to be cosmetic, but people are willing to pay money out of their own pockets for the end results.

The prosthodontist profession can be summed up by saying that these individuals get involved with all types of replacements related to teeth. They recognize people's needs and restore or replace teeth as necessary. Sometimes their work is done alone, but they have also been known to work on teams that establish solutions to dental problems. They understand the importance of people's smiles and devote their careers to the maintenance of those smiles.

Education and training

In addition to a science-based undergraduate degree and a doctoral degree from a dental school, prosthodontists need to undergo training in specific areas of their profession including that for dental implants, bridges, crowns, and dentures. After this training, they must take and pass an examination by The American Board of Prosthodontics before they are allowed to legally practice. A final indication of their skills is the requirement of re-certification every eight years to insure their awareness and use of up-to-date practices.

Orthodontist

Description

"Orthodontist" is a word commonly used in the households of families all over the world because so many kids wear braces on their teeth. In fact, as far as many adolescents are concerned, orthodontists are the most well-known and notorious type of dentist. Kids do not normally like to wear braces, but later in life, they usually appreciate the fact that they were forced to do so because their teeth look good to themselves and others.

Unfortunately, people with unattractive smiles and damaged teeth indicate poor dental care that others sometimes translate into poor care of other aspects of life. This is a form of bias that, while very unfortunate and not fair, does occur and can prevent people from getting jobs, attracting mates, and playing important roles in social and work related situations.

The effects and notoriety of orthodontists could be discussed in much more detail, but that is not the focus of this book. In terms of job function, these dentists are best known for moving, extracting, and encasing teeth so they fit properly and look attractive in people's mouths. In a sense, their work overlaps that of cosmic dentists, but the results take a lot longer to transpire.

Education and training

Orthodontists typically complete a science-based undergraduate degree, finish dental school, and undergo specialized training to sharpen their skills   This training can be quite intense since people expect al lot from orthodontists...especially when their kids are the patients and their dental insurance does not cover all of the costs. Experienced orthodontists watch over the work of trainees for about three years to insure they are knowledgeable and skilled before entering practice on their own. After the training has been completed, aspiring orthodontists need to take an examination administered by The American Board of Orthodontics. They must pass the written and clinical portions of the exam before they obtain their license to practice.

Endodontist

Description

Endodontists diagnose, treat, and prevent injury and disease to the internal areas of teeth. These specialists use microscopes to examine and treat the center of a tooth without doing damage to the internal structure. One of their most common job functions is to perform root canals. General dentists also perform root canals, but only if they are simple. Anything complex is referred to an endodontist who is often times employed in the same office.

Essentially, a root canal is needed when the root becomes contaminated with bacteria. It involves removing the diseased pulp from the center of the tooth while keeping the tooth intact. The root is then cleaned, sanitized, and filled with a substance that promotes healing and prevents future infection or disease. Many times a crown is needed to strengthen the tooth since its core has been removed, but the tooth does not have to be extracted; thereby preventing an open gap or further treatment such as a bridge or an implant.

Over the past decade, endodontists have probably evolved more than any of the other types of dentists. They are not quite as popular as general dentists or orthodontists, but their presence is quickly becoming known to people due to the demand for their services. Quite simply, people who have complex root problems need endodontists.

Education and training

Like other dentists, endodontists typically obtain a science-based undergraduate degree and then move into dental school. After earning their doctoral degree, their specialization requires additional training in the areas of tooth root operations, microsurgery, dental emergencies, and trauma management. Tooth root operations and microsurgery are needed because the delicate areas of internal teeth are targeted, and dental emergencies and trauma management training are necessary because patients are often in great pain and under the stress of losing teeth. This training is intense and adds at least two more years to the licensing process. After finishing the training program, aspiring endodontists need to pass an examination by the American Board of Endodontics, After passing this exam, they become licensed to practice.

Interestingly, all endodontic training is not the same. Some training heavily emphasizes the use of a microscope for analysis, treatment, and surgery while other training promotes good lighting and the use of magnifiers or, in some cases, the naked eye. Additionally, three dimensional imaging assessments are becoming popular in many endodontic practices that conduct training, but other practices have no familiarity with the concept so they do not use it.

Cosmetic dentist

Description

It must first be noted that The American Dental Association does not formally recognize cosmetic dentistry as a specialized area of dentistry. However, despite this lack of formal recognition, some dental professionals devote their practice to cosmetic procedures and promote themselves as cosmetic dentists.

Cosmetic dentists overlap responsibilities with prosthodontists. Both of these professionals are concerned with healthy teeth and gums, but cosmetic dentists typically focus more on aesthetics rather than health and practicality. For example, cosmetic procedures include bleaching teeth to get them whiter and extracting silver fillings for replacement with fillings that match the color of the teeth.   Both of these procedures are not necessary for health reasons, but people like the end results and are willing to pay for them...even though they are not covered by many dental insurance plans. Quite simply, most people want a nice smile because it is attractive and it is one of the first and most prominent features noticed by others.

Cosmetic dentists work to improve people's appearance, but this does not mean that they are not concerned about those people's health and well-being. They want their patients to look good and feel good from alterations made to their teeth. Internal pain and suffering are not acceptable to these professionals, regardless of the eye appeal of their patients' smiles.

Education and training

Cosmetic dentists usually obtain an undergraduate degree with an emphasis on chemistry and microbiology before they apply and are accepted into dental school. During and after dental school, they receive training on improving people's smiles by repairing chips, adding veneers, bonding teeth, inserting bridges, and a variety of other aesthetic procedures. The extensive education and training they undergo allow them to gain a better understanding of the field where they intend to practice.

Since cosmetic dentists are not technically a specialty of dentistry, they follow the same basic path to certification as general dentists. Once their training is completed, they must take and pass an examination administered by The American Board of General Dentistry, and then they are able to obtain a license and begin their practice.

Oral dentist

Oral dentists address maxillofacial (mouth, face, and jaw) related problems. More specifically, they diagnose and treat diseases, defects, deformities, and injuries that are beyond the skills of general dentistry. Most interestingly, they look for cysts, tumors, and cancerous areas of the mouth, face, head, and neck.

Oral dentists are unique due to the fact that they are further divided into sub-categories including:

Oral pathologist

Description

As the name implies, oral pathologists focus on pathological issues. More specifically, they diagnose and treat malignant and benign pathology of the mouth, head, face, neck, and jaw. They explore areas such as salivary glands and facial muscles to find sources of problems. They also look at skin, especially that around the mouth, to find the causes of diseases with the hope that they are treatable.

Oral pathologists play a big role in dentistry because they focus on "why" something happened. Other types of dentists tend to treat the problems the find, rather than research where they came from and why the occurred.

Quite possibly the most important aspect of oral pathologists' work is prevention. When they discover why something happened, they keep digging until the determine how to stop it from happening again. These investigative measures are unique because other dentists focus the majority of their time resolving problems that have already occurred rather than conducting preventative research.

Education and training

The standard science-based undergraduate degree and dental school completion are required before undergoing specialized training in the field under the watchful eye of a mentor. This training takes about three years to complete, and then the aspiring oral pathologists need to take an examination administered by The American Board of Oral and Maxillofacial Pathology. Upon completing and passing this exam, these individuals are able to obtain their license and practice.

Oral radiologist

Description

Oral radiologists combine radiology and dentistry so they can create and interpret radiographic images such as MRI scans. These images are then used to diagnose and treat diseases, deformities, and injuries of the mouth, face, and jaws.

Oral radiologists differentiate themselves from other dentists because they have an in-depth understanding of machines, such as X-rays, and the tools used with those machines. They are increasingly becoming more popular in areas such as sports where injuries to the face can occur.

Education and training

In addition to a science-based undergraduate diploma and a dental degree, oral radiologists need to undergo training in the field that typically requires a one or two year residency with skilled mentors. This training is very technology-based since dental equipment and machinery is continually changed as new discoveries are made. After the residency, aspiring oral radiologists need to pass an examination by The American Board of Oral and Maxillofacial Surgery (ABOMS) before they can become licensed to practice.

Oral surgeon

Description

Recognized for being a specialty of medicine and dentistry, oral surgeons are probably the most popular sub-category of oral dentistry because they are known for their surgical abilities all over the world. They primarily treat diseased areas, defected areas, and injurious areas of the face, neck, bone, and jaws. Specific treatments include treatment of cleft palates and bone-fused tooth implants.

The demand for oral surgeons is increasing as people become more and more concerned about their dental health. Never before has so much attention been paid to surgical repair of dental issues that result from injury, possibly because lawsuits and worker's compensation often pay for the work that needs to be done, but also for the longevity of oral health.

Education and training

These dentists start by completing a science-based undergraduate degree. They then enter dental school and complete the same requirements as other dentists. However, oral surgery requires a wealth of knowledge and skills, so additional training is needed after dental school. This training involves general surgery, anesthesia, and internal medicine, and it takes about four years to complete. After the training, aspiring oral surgeons must take The Oral Certifying Examination administered by The American Board of Oral and Maxillofacial Surgery. Upon passing this exam, these individuals are able to obtain a license and practice.

As you can see, there are quite a few specializations in dentistry. This is particularly interesting because dentists only treat the head, face, mouth, and neck. The rest of the body is treated by medical doctors. In fact, some dentists overlap territories with medical doctors including those who focus on ears, noses, throats and, less frequently, eyes.

Please keep in mind that all examination requirements are subject to change. Officials strive to incorporate modern dentistry into the licensing process, and exams often need to be updated or replaced as they become outdated. These changes are understandable because people want the best dental care available for themselves and their families.

Now that you have a basic understanding of the major specializations of dentists, let's move on to a short discussion on the future of dentistry as a whole.

Future

It should be noted that, regardless of the number of specialties, dentists often overlap responsibilities. For example, general dentists can do cosmetic work such as bleaching teeth, but they often choose to send patients to cosmetic dentists who have more specialized training. Similarly, oral surgeons can do endodontic work such as root canals, but they often refer patients to endodontists for more sensitive or complex internal tooth issues.

Specialized care is somewhat of a luxury that was not available in the past because one dentist did all of the work. This has changed because people want better dental care, and it will continue to evolve in the future. Dental services will always be required, and specialized sub-categories will continue to grow in numbers. This growth is because specialists are able to provide better services, but, unfortunately, it is also due to the lawsuits that patients file for incompetence or malpractice against dentists who lack specific knowledge.

Summary

Dentists play a critical role in many people's lives. They are often thought of as only working on people's teeth, but in reality, they identify and correct health problems related to the mouth, face, neck, and head. They are rarely thought about until they are needed, and then patients can think of little else...especially if those patients are in pain.

This book is part of a series that provides short and simple explanations of different professions. It focuses on dentists by breaking down different types, examining specializations, and discussing education and training requirements. It uses language and terminology that is understood by the average person, and it is written for easy comprehension at all reader levels.

Congratulations! You now know more about dentists...professionals that everyone needs to see at some point in their lives.

Social Workers

Short and Simple Explanation Series
Book 2

Louis Bevoc

Published by
NutriNiche System LLC

Louis Bevoc books...simple explanations of complex subjects

Introduction

This is the second book in a series of short and simple explanations of professions. For every book, the profession is described along with a discussion on the required education and training. These books are written so people can inform and educate themselves on various professions without having to understand difficult language or complex terminology...which is the underlying philosophy of all Louis Bevoc books.

Social workers are professionals concerned with the mental and physical well-being of individuals, families, groups, and communities. They are employed in a wide variety of settings including colleges, hospitals, nursing homes, medical clinics, mental health facilities, community centers, government agencies, and substance abuse programs. Essentially, their job is to help people feel better about themselves, their families, their friends, their jobs, and their environments.

Social work has been around for quite a while. Its roots were established in Europe in the mid-1900's when private organizations and charities helped impoverished people become self-sufficient in terms of basic needs. A lot was done during this time and it was a rather slow progression, but it essentially boiled down to convincing government leaders and politicians to empower and liberate poor people through social actions. In short, it was all about people helping people with charitable contributions.

European social actions paved the way for the profession of social work as it is known today. This profession is grounded in many different areas of the social sciences including psychology, sociology, economics, law, and political science. These areas can be subdivided further, such as psychology-related work being broken down into helping is diverse because it addresses a variety of different needs.

Social workers are unique because they can work with one person, a group of people, or an entire community of people depending on the situation. They can also work alone, with other social workers, or with people from different professions such as nursing and psychology. However, regardless of the nature of their colleagues or the size of their audience, social workers typically have a goal of implementing some type of individual, group, or community change as exemplified below.

Individual

A social worker is assigned to a man who has a drug problem and is trying not to relapse. First, she assesses the needs of the man by considering factors such as his mental health, physical condition, type of addiction, and length of time addicted.

After she has an idea of the man's needs, the social worker formulates a plan to get him into a treatment program designed to help him. Once in the program, she monitors the man's behavior to assure he is not relapsing. Monitoring can consist of simple observation or something more detailed such as drug testing. If the man appears to be doing well, then the social worker will attempt to find him some type of employment so he can change his outlook on life and view himself as a productive member of society.

Group

A social worker is assigned to a single-parent family where the three children are not attending classes at their school. She assesses the situation by visiting the children's school to see how they are viewed in the eyes of teachers and administrators, and she also goes to their home to learn more about the environment in which they are being raised.

After the social worker understands the family's situation, she implements an educational program that emphasizes the importance of parenthood and the value of education. This program offers support groups and financial aid to the struggling parent and establishes direction for the children. Once the family begins the program, the social worker monitors their progress by checking the children's school attendance records and asking questions regarding their behavior.

Community

A social worker is assigned to an entire community of homeless people squatting in abandoned houses in a dilapidated inner-city area. He assesses the situation to see if this community has their basic needs met including food, shelter, and clothing.

After determining the needs of the community, the social worker offers homeless shelters and job placement programs to everyone so they have an opportunity to get out of their current financial situation and move into better living conditions. She then monitors the involvement of community members in the program, their success for finding employment, and their progress moving out of the abandoned homes.

Obviously, the above examples are greatly oversimplified, but they give a basic idea of how social workers implement, maintain, and monitor change for the betterment of the people involved. Without this type of intervention, social problems would escalate and people would suffer.

Many social workers begin their quest for change with grassroots-based movements, meaning they start with a small group of people and work toward affecting larger groups of people using bottom-to-top decision making and actions. They encourage everyone involved to take some sort of action for the cause. For example, a social worker's group of seven volunteers attempts to get more companies to donate food or money to local homeless shelters. To accomplish this task, each member solicits local businesses via in-person visits and drops off literature detailing the need for the help of those businesses. Once the businesses start to give, they become part of the movement and increase awareness for the need for money and food.

In short, social work feeds off several different areas of social science. Social workers are employed in the profession of social work, and their goals revolve around promoting change that helps people feel better and become self-sufficient. They practice in a variety of different institutions and settings that include health facilities, homes for the aged, government agencies, universities, and independent businesses. They support people by acting as their advocates for humane practices, policies, and procedures that promote happiness and independence.

Types

Similar to other professions, social workers can be broken down into sub-categories based on the work that they perform. These sub-categories are based on several different factors including the organization, culture, environment, economic structure, and people involved and they are listed below.

Please keep in mind that this list is not all-encompassing and arguments could be made for adding or deleting sub-categories, but it gives a good basic idea of the types of social work that take place all over the world.

Medical

Description

Medical social work is a busy occupation due to the multi-tasking of jobs that must take place to achieve success. These professionals need to be able to apply social theories to real-world situations while counseling and consoling people in situations that can be very serious. For example, a sickness that takes over a community requires a lot of work, patience, and understanding in order to deal with the differing personalities of the victims. Add to this the fact that government agencies, physicians, nurses, and politicians are involved, and it is rather easy to see what the social workers are up against.

The goal of medical social workers is to bring about positive change in regard to health-related issues. They advise people by referring them to proven methods that repair and improve processes that have been broken. They restructure and reform individuals, groups, and communities in order to begin the healing process. They monitor the situations they create and make the necessary changes to keep those situations heading in the right direction.

Medical social workers are unique because they are sometimes dealing with life or death situations that, if not brought under control, can spread to people other than those currently affected. They are not doctors, but they are involved in the health and longevity of their clients.

Most medical social workers are employed in hospitals or outpatient healthcare centers. Since they understand the needs of people, they often work as therapists, counselors, and case managers for their clients. Their work can involve something as simple as directing and guiding people to the resources they need to help them overcome their health-related issues or it can be much more complex such as diagnosing and/or treating psychological problems. In short, medical social workers help people change their health for the betterment of themselves and others.

Education and Training

An undergraduate degree in social work (BSW) allows people to become medical social workers, but the higher up positions are usually reserved for those who possess master's degrees in social work (MSW). The programs for these degrees allow for specific concentrations within including health care.

In order to be licensed, medical social workers need to take examinations that are administered by the Association of Social Work Boards. However, the licensing requirements also call for a few years training under an experienced social worker in order to gain real-world experience. Once the training is completed and the exam has been passed, the social workers can obtain a license to practice.

After becoming licensed, medical social workers can add other certifications to their portfolio which are voluntary and indicate a specialization in a particular area of medical social work. These certifications enhance social workers as professionals, provide them with job security, and promote their visibility in the field of their chosen career.

School

Description

All responsibilities of school social workers cannot be addressed in the scope of this book, especially since some of these responsibilities overlap with those of family social workers. However, it can be said that school social workers function as a link between schools and parents to relay the positive or negative progress of the children being monitored. This progress refers to the children's academic success or failure as well as their socialization, behavior, and mental states inside and outside their classrooms.

When classroom related problems with children are discovered, school social workers react by taking immediate action or referring the parents, teachers, and administrators to resources that can help provide solutions prevent reoccurrences. Immediate action includes counseling where the affected children have an opportunity to discuss their problems and develop their own resolution strategies. Counseling has worked well in the past because students realize the fact that they have caused some or many of the problems they are experiencing. This self-reflection brings about behavioral change that helps the students adjust to their situations. Examples of behavior that can change with counseling include students' attendance issues, communication abilities, and socialization skills.

In addition to counseling, school social workers also educate parents and school staffs with educational opportunities that promote understanding of children's behavior. Awareness is important for prevention of problems, and awareness starts with education.

Last, but certainly not least, school social workers engage in risk management and crisis management. They assess the risks of students behaving improperly based on their education and experience, and they work to prevent problems before they incubate and grow. However, some problems still transpire regardless of risk the risk management conducted, so school social workers need to implement crisis management plans to stop students' from damaging themselves and others.

Education and Training

Similar to every other type of social worker, school social workers require a minimum of a bachelor's degree in social work (BSW). However, the BSW is typically not enough to move into the higher school social work positions because a master's degree (MSW) is required. However, regardless of which degree is earned, school social workers also need to undergo training in their field under the watchful eyes of an experienced mentor. When the training is complete, school social workers are able to obtain a license to practice.

If they so desire, school social workers can continue their education and become certified in specific areas after becoming licensed. These programs elevate social them to a higher status among their peers through certifications that are obtained upon completion of the required work. The certifications do not necessarily mean the social worker will get promoted or receive a pay increase, but they do enhance their professional careers.

Military

Description

These social workers are unique. They differentiate themselves from other social workers because they work with a specific portion of the population known as the military. Almost everyone in the United States, including children, knows that the military consists of the Army, Navy, Air Force, and Marines. These individuals are real-world heroes, but, unlike make-believe heroes, they experience mental and physical pain...and that pain sometimes requires the services of military social workers.

Social workers employed in a military capacity work with current and former members of the armed services along with their families. Sometimes working with the families is more important than working with the military personnel experiencing pain because those families need to provide constant support, especially when that pain is psychological.

Common mental health problems experienced by military personnel include anxiety, post-traumatic stress, and other emotionally charged issues of the mind. Often times these problems stem from combat action, but other factors such as substance abuse or depression also contribute to the cause.

Military social workers can be active-duty members, government workers, or employees of private practices. Active duty members with master's degrees (MSW) are often commissioned officers who are paid by the military to act as social workers who service the needs of their fellow members. Government social workers come from a few different agencies with one of the most common agencies being the US Department of Veterans Affairs...which is also the biggest employer of social workers possessing an advanced degree. Social workers who come from private practices often own them or work for a group of other professionals. However, regardless of where they are employed, military social workers must be ready to diagnose and treat physical, mental, and emotional issues with active members, veterans, and their families.

Education and Training

A minimum of a master's degree (MSW) is required education for social workers in all branches of the armed forces because these individuals need to service many different people who have a wide variety of problems. Quite simply, military officials believe an undergraduate degree by itself is not enough schooling to handle the responsibilities involved.

Education and training requirements are not uniform, and they differ from one branch of the military to another. For example, the Army has no experience or training requirements but Army social workers must be licensed to practice before being hired or commissioned. The Navy also has no experience or training requirements, but social workers must commit at least three years of their lives to active duty. The Air Force is the most demanding in terms of experience and training because social workers are required to have at least two years of clinical experience or they must complete the Air Force Social Work Internship Program.

Please note that there are age rules for getting into any branch of the military. These rules typically require a person to be no younger than 18 (or sometimes 21) and no older than 41 (approximately). Age requirements can be waived in certain situations such as wartime, but they are in place and they can limit younger and older social workers from getting hired or commissioned.

Community

Description

As their name suggests, community social workers service communities of people for improvement purposes. The essentially interact with clients similar to the way school social workers interact, but they work with large groups rather than small groups of people. These large groups (or communities) are established for several reasons including:

- People share common interests such as the members of a classic car club.
- People share similar heritages such as the members of a Native-American community center.
- People share common causes such as the members of a breast cancer survivor group.
- People share geographical linkages such as the members of a condominium association.
- People share business relationships such as the members of a union.

Community social workers understand that communities contain people with differing religion, race, gender, and socio-economic status…who also have different experiences, viewpoints, beliefs, and values. This diversity is good for communities because "variety is the spice of life," but it can also lead to conflict. Conflict is beneficial if it is functional, but dysfunctional conflict leads to people focusing on position rather than principle; thereby creating the risk that people will be attacked instead of problems. If personal attacks take place, then people stop communicating with each other and communities break down.

In a nutshell, community social workers improve communities by bringing internal and external issues to the forefront and resolving them with the help of everyone involved. An example of an internal issue is conflict between people within the community such as that mentioned in the previous paragraph. An example of an external issue is getting leaders and politicians to pay attention to the breast cancer survivor group listed in the bullet points of this section so change can be initiated. Specific tasks of community social workers include establishing member rules and regulations, writing grants, acting as advocates, establishing outreach programs, working with local politicians, and conducting research on alternative solutions to problems.

Community social workers are similar to other social workers because they work to bring about positive change. However, unlike other social workers, the change initiated by community social workers occurs among large groups of people who share something in common.

Education and Training

All social workers need to complete an undergraduate degree in social work (BSW) so they can become generalists and work in their profession in the public or private sector. Often times, these individuals accept government positions at the local, state, or federal level. However, a master's degree in social work (MSW) is required for higher level positions in the field. If the MSW is clinically based, then the social worker can counsel others, conduct research and perform studies within the community.

Regardless of the degree, some communities require training before hiring social workers. This training makes good sense because community social work requires a wealth of knowledge, and, other than education, training is the best way to acquire that knowledge. The training can last a few years and it must be overseen by an experienced community social worker.

Mental health (including substance abuse)

Description

Many people associate social workers with helping those who have mental health issues. This association is accurate, but, after reading this book, it is rather obvious that they have many other responsibilities.

Unfortunately, many people suffer from mental problems. Some of these problems are self-inflicted, such as drug abuse, but others are brought on by factors outside of people's control, such as depression. However, regardless of the cause, mental health problems need to be treated; thereby validating the importance of the services provided by mental health social workers.

Essentially, the role of mental health care social workers is to intervene after problems have been discovered. They provide therapy, counseling, and education on resources available for treatment and prevention of the mental issues.   In this role, they often work with other types of social workers to help people in need. For example, they might temporarily work with military social workers to treat Army soldiers who have returned from combat if the number of soldiers is excessive. The might also work with school social workers to help the many families of students who have survived a school shooting.

In short, mental health social workers help people with mental and psychological issues regardless of where those people live, what they do, or what they have experienced. There are licensed to treat problems related to the mind which, unfortunately, affect a wide variety of people.

Education and Training

Most mental health social workers must have an undergraduate (BSW) and master's (MSW) in social work. Their MSW revolves around clinical social work, but it also incorporates modern technology and various aspects of research. In terms of training, these social workers typically undergo some type of internship with exposure to clinical work before being able to obtain their license to practice.

Administrative (including research)

Description

Administrative social workers are different from other types of social workers because they focus on the overall puzzle rather than individual pieces. In other words, they have a macro-focus rather than a micro-focus of the field in general. For example, an administrative social worker heading up the Health and Human Services department of Ohio must consider the needs of every person in the state including those in rural and urban areas. This consideration will take into account many factors that are not acknowledged by social workers in the inner city of Cleveland, but those factors are critical for the overall effectiveness of the department.

Administrative social workers also look at the future more than what is happening now because they need to make decisions that affect the status of social work later on. For example, they might work on budgets for departments that will affect the resources available for their departments over the next two years. It takes thought and planning to visualize what is going to happen during this time period, and decisions made will have a lasting impact on people, projects, and materials.

In short, administrative social workers are leaders who must understand human behavior and designate the appropriate resources and services when issues arise. Like it or not, they need to take a political and business approach to problem-solving, unlike other social workers who view human needs above everything else.

Administrative social workers almost always require a master's degree in social work (MSW) with a focus on policy and procedures, administration, activism, and community. Training is valuable, but it is not always a major factor because these professionals gain important knowledge as they move up the hierarchical ladder. The learning process must be this way because administrative social workers need to develop their own leadership style and that style is based on workplace experiences rather than training.

Future

The future of social work can be summed up by saying that "with little doubt, it will be around." However, everything is not always as easy as it appears, so this statement needs to be qualified with some words of caution. Consider the following factors for a better understanding of how social work will be affected as it moves forward in time:

- If history continues to repeat itself, and it likely will, then wealth will separate people and society will contain financial "haves" and "have-nots." Individuals who have money do not have to worry about their basic needs being met, but, unfortunately, the same cannot be said for those who lack financial resources. In short, money does not buy happiness, but lack of it creates misery and a need for social workers.
- Money also plays a role when social work programs fall under the control of government agencies. When budgets are exceeded or local, state, and federal funding runs out, those programs need to be suspended or eliminated. Suspension of elimination raises questions about the value of those programs; thereby questioning the value of social work as a profession.
- Regardless of wealth, there will be people with health needs. Money cannot correct all health-related issues, especially if those issues involve mental health. When people cannot help themselves, regardless of their financial standing, they require the outside intervention of others...and many times those others are social workers.
- Families will always be broken apart by divorce, death, lack of resources, or simple desertion. When this happens, some family members have trouble coping internally with their situations so they turn to the outside world of social work for help...and this need supports the value of social work.
- As the world moves forward, some people believe in and push for independence though self-imposed actions rather than leaning on others. In other words, they expect people to "pull themselves up by their own bootstraps." This thinking questions the need for social work because those who use it become dependent on the help they are receiving. Over time, the cycle of "need and help" can become ever-present and ongoing; thereby making social work a cause of the problem rather than a solution for it.

As you can see from the above bullet points, social work will be needed in the future. However, the value of that need will be questioned, as is the case for many different types of social programs. In short, social work will come under scrutiny, and the people who scrutinize it will never stop voicing their concerns.

Summary

Social workers play an active and necessary role in society by providing for those who lack the ability or resources to provide for themselves and their families. These professionals are part of a group that can honestly state that they work toward bettering individuals, groups, and communities. Without social work, people would suffer mentally and physically and governments would experience problems that they are not equipped to handle and resolve.

This book provides a basic description of the profession of social work. It examines social work in general, breaks down specific types of social workers, and discusses the education and training required to become a social worker. The text is educational and informational, and it is written for easy understanding at all reader levels.

Congratulations! You now understand more about social work...a profession that will be around as long as people need help improving themselves and their situations.

Skilled Trades
In Manufacturing
Short and Simple Explanation Series
Book 3

Louis Bevoc

Published by
NutriNiche System LLC

Louis Bevoc books...simple explanations of complex subjects

Introduction

This is the third book in a series of short and simple explanations of professions. For every book, the profession is described along with a discussion on the required education and training. These books are written so people can inform and educate themselves on various professions without having to understand difficult language or complex terminology...which is the underlying philosophy of all Louis Bevoc books.

Since the 1960s, the trend for young people who graduate high school has been to get a college education. The thinking behind this is that a college degree yields a return-on-investment that cannot be achieved via other types of training or experience. The increase in high school grads choosing to go to college has prevented many of them from pursuing careers in skilled trades. Classrooms are preferred over apprenticeships, meaning students pay upfront for education that can be used later on rather than earning money while learning from on the job experience.   Interestingly, skilled tradespeople often earn more money than college graduates, but the perception and physical work involved leads to many young people staying away from skilled trades as a career choice.

This book focuses on many different types of skilled trades in manufacturing including:

Electrical
Plumbing
Welding
Heating and cooler
Machinery
Carpentry
Tool & Die
Model makers

Each trade is described and exemplified using real-world application and the training and education requirements necessary for certification are discussed. This information helps readers understand the trade in layman's terms and allows them to see it in action. The goal is for readers to develop basic knowledge about all of the trades discussed, so let's get started.

Electrical

The following pertains to skilled tradespeople who are employed in manufacturing plants in an electrical capacity:

Description

Electrical skilled tradespeople are commonly known as electricians. These workers specialize in electrical wiring of plants, machines, equipment, and mobile devices such as floor jacks and forklifts. Their skills are in high demand for production facilities, and that is why they are one of the most popular types of trades in manufacturing.

Electricians have a wide variety of responsibilities in manufacturing plants, but they are often charged with installations, upgrades, and repairs of the plant, equipment, and machinery. In this role, they often function as project managers by overseeing all electrical aspects of a job. In short, they are directly involved in the labor and management aspects of many types of electrical work.

Education and training

Electricians are usually unionized employees who start as apprentices, work their way into a journeyman status, and then become master electricians. Typically, they are apprentices for three years or more, learning the trade on the job from more experienced electricians. During their apprenticeship, they earn money, but not as much money as journeymen electricians. Apprentice electricians are also required to log classroom hours. This combination of work experience and classroom education prepares them for the certification they need to be officially licensed as journeyman electricians. Without this certification, they cannot perform many of the job functions that manufacturing plants require.

Master electricians are the highest level of the trade. To become a master, journeymen electricians need about ten years of on-the-job experience and also must pass a written exam. This is not an easy task because it requires working knowledge of the National Electric Code (NEC). The NEC is quite extensive and encompasses a wealth of information, but electricians who understand it truly are prepared to take on the challenges found in manufacturing facilities.

Example

Hector is a master electrician at a paper mill. The plant manager decides to put an addition on the plant for greater production capacity, and he needs all electrical wiring in the addition to meet local code. Hector understands the code, and he oversees all wiring so that it is compliant. This allows the plant manager to focus on production and quality related issues rather than worry about the addition passing the electrical inspection of local authorities.

Plumbing

The following pertains to skilled tradespeople who are employed in manufacturing plants in a plumbing capacity:

Description

Plumbing skilled tradespeople are typically known as plumbers. They can also be pipefitters, steamfitters, and boilermakers...but these trades sometimes have skills other than or in addition to plumbing. Pipefitters, steamfitters, and boilermakers often work as plumbers, but plumbers focus on low-pressure piping systems that convey water while pipefitters, steamfitters, and boilermakers work with higher pressure systems for moving steam, chemicals, and fuel. However, pipefitters, steamfitters, and boilermakers might not have the same plumbing skills as plumbers because their jobs are not specifically geared toward plumbing problems.

Plumbers are valuable to manufactures because water, steam, chemicals, and fuel must be moved via lines of piping in virtually every plant. Plumbers keep these lines open; thereby avoiding hindrance of production processes. They also work on sanitary lines, potable water structures, and sewerage systems. Backed up drains in production facilities can lead to many different problems including plant, equipment, and machinery damage. Plugged drains have even been known to bring manufacturers to a complete halt, so it is rather obvious that plumbers are "worth their weight in gold" in these situations.

Plumbers handle small and big problems in manufacturing plants. In the same day, they might fix the faucet of a sink in the employee break room and then move on to repair a broken water main that has the potential to cease plant operations. Other responsibilities include reading drawings, relocating lines, installing apparatus, threading and soldering pipes, testing for leaks, working on drainage systems, and adhering to sanitary requirements. They must also be aware of safety standards, building regulations, and legal regulations when working in manufacturing facilities.

Education and training

It takes many years to become a knowledgeable plumber because the ability to troubleshoot problems and develop cost-effective solutions is essential. Training for this trade is best done on the job and, although there is no federal licensing available, state and local governments often require plumbers to be licensed for the work they perform. Unfortunately, some people believe plumbers are not governed by any rules, but this is simply not true.

Example

Edwardo is a plumber at a meat processing facility. There is a drain backup in the smokehouse area, and production has been shut down until the clog is removed and the drain flows freely. Edwardo understands that the clog is east of the drain, not west of it, because he understands the flow of the sewage lines running underneath the plant floor. He wastes little time as he runs his "snake" into the pipe 50 feet east of the drain. The clog is removed, and the drain begins to function properly due to Edwardo's knowledge of the sewer pipe system running under the plant.

Welding

The following pertains to skilled tradespeople who are employed in manufacturing plants in a welding capacity:

Description

Welding skilled tradespeople are typically known as welders. They use welding machinery to fuse materials together for bonding purposes. Most people associate welding with metal, but other materials welded include polymers and plastics.

Welders often have a sub-skill within their trade. For example, a metal welder might focus on stainless steel due to the challenges involved with this type of welding. Stainless steel has specific properties that vary from other metals, and many stainless welds are required to be smooth for use in food or pharmaceutical applications. Aluminum welders also possess a sub-skill because the metal is soft and requires skill not to damage. The low melting point and high thermal conductivity of aluminum can lead to burn through of the metal unless the welder has the necessary knowledge.

Welders are valuable to manufacturers because their skills are needed for the wide variety of machines necessary for production. They are capable of fabrication or repair, and their work is critical for systems and processes to operate smoothly and effectively. They are always needed in production geared facilities because machinery is necessary to generate a high volume of products, and high volume is the key to profitability for many manufacturers.

Welders are often charged with installing equipment and machinery. They are typically responsible for the design of the projects that involve them; thereby requiring them to have a practical working knowledge of physics and mathematics. They are also responsible for making sure safety and sanitary standards are adhered to, and they need to do their jobs with limited input from others. Some welders work on teams in manufacturing plants while others perform their jobs by themselves, but it is essential that they are all able to accomplish their goals and objectives without direct supervision.

Education and training

Training for welders can be done via a postsecondary associate degree, educational certificate, or apprenticeship that involves several months of on the job training under the supervision of an established welding mentor. Associate degrees in welding are offered by many accredited universities while educational certificates are offered by schools that specialize in welding. However, many welders prefer to learn the trade under the watchful eye of a skilled welder, and this is enough to get them jobs in many manufacturing plants.

Example

Devon is a welder at automotive parts manufacturer. The company is revamping one of its production lines so it can handle a larger volume of products, and Devon is the lead welder on the project. She has two other welders working under her, and her team needs to weld a series of conveyors so they are able to handle the increased flow of product. She coordinates every aspect of the welding, including assigning the other team members jobs and setting deadlines for completion. In this role, Devon is a welder and a lead worker which earns her a ten percent higher pay rate than any other welder at the plant.

Heating and cooling

The following pertains to skilled tradespeople who are employed in manufacturing plants in a heating and cooling capacity:

Description

These individuals are often employed as technologists for environmental comfort in buildings and vehicles. They work on heating, ventilation, and air conditioning systems (HVAC) in people's homes and cars. In this capacity, they are usually directly hired by homeowners or car owners to do specialized work involving repair or service.

In manufacturing, heating and cooling skilled tradespeople typically work on furnaces, refrigeration systems, and air conditioners. Their service might be as simple as adding Freon to an air conditioner or it might as complex as installing an entirely new refrigeration system.

Similar to welders, heating and cooling tradespeople often have a specific skill. One person's skill might be heating while another's is cooling, and some specialize in indoor work while others focus on outdoor jobs.

Heating and cooling tradespeople handle any job related to heating and cooling in manufacturing. They might work on a furnace for the offices or they might install a refrigeration system for a 1,000,000 square foot plant. They designate refrigerant types, determine capacities (tonnage), create designs, and oversee projects. They need to understand the basic principles of mechanical engineering, thermodynamics, heat transfer, and refrigeration. They often work in teams, but it is essential that they are able to work alone as many jobs do not require multiple technicians.

Education and training

Training for heating and cooling people is done in specialized schools and on the job under the supervision of an established tradesperson. Certificates can vary, but they often are as follows:

- *Type I Certificate* - For the installation, repair, and service of most small appliances in homes or offices (window air conditioners, refrigerators, freezer, vending machines, etc.).

- *Type II Certificate* - For the installation, repair, and service of high-pressure refrigerant equipment (heat pumps, central air conditioners, commercial refrigeration, etc.).

- *Type III Certificate* - For the installation, repair, and service of low-pressure refrigerant equipment in industry.

- *Type IV Certificate (Universal)* - For the installation, repair, service, and disposition of equipment containing any type of refrigerant.

Example

Rodriquez is employed at a heating and cooling company that services a metal casting foundry. Heating is a critical aspect of the processes at the foundry, and Rodriquez specialty is heating equipment. He visits the plant every Wednesday to perform routine service work, and he is on call 24/7 for equipment malfunctions and breakdowns.

Most of the jobs at the foundry can be handled by Rodriquez without any help, but he has two other technicians who are familiar with the foundry's process if they are needed for a team effort. The foundry understands the importance of having Rodriquez available at a moment's notice, so they pay a monthly retainer fee for his services.

Machinery

For simplification purposes, this book breaks down machinery tradespeople into two distinct subcategories known as millwrights and machinists. In manufacturing, millwrights fabricate, install, maintain, and repair machinery while machinists operate those machines to make products. The following examines both subcategories of machinery tradespeople who are employed in manufacturing:

Millwrights

Description

Millwrights typically perform work on machinery in manufacturing plants. This machinery is usually stationary (such as presses and mold makers) rather than mobile (such as floor jacks and forklifts), and the work involves installation, service, moving, or repair.

Millwrights' jobs are usually less specific than some of the other tradespeople, so they need to be quite versatile. They must read service manuals and schematics, implement preventive and predictive maintenance, align mechanical equipment, operate rigging equipment, and tack weld on a moment's notice. They must also understand the basics of electronics, pneumatics, and hydraulics and be able to work without direct supervision. Last, but certainly not least, millwrights sometimes need to perform work in high places, so they should not be afraid of height.

Education and training

Schools offer training and certificates for millwrights, but this type of tradesperson also learns under the watchful eyes of an experienced journeyman. Formal apprentice programs that last several years are often required by unions and contractors before a person earns the rank of a journeyman. Once that rank is achieved, millwrights are authorized to work without direct supervision.

Example

Terrance is a millwright in an automotive assembly plant. He and four other millwrights have been assigned the responsibility of installing a stamping press on the production floor. His specific job on this project is to make sure the machine is aligned correctly so it functions properly. He does not necessarily need the help of the other millwrights, but he can use their help if they are needed.

Terrance does not have any major weaknesses as a millwright, and he is capable of performing every type of task that falls under his job function. His experience and knowledge make him a valuable asset to the automotive assembly plant for a wide variety of different projects.

Machinists

Description

Similar to millwrights, machinist positions are often defined by unions. However, their major job function is to operate machinery in manufacturing plants. This machinery is usually stationary (such as presses and mold makers) rather than mobile (such as floor jacks and forklifts).

Machinists' jobs are often very specific because they work on the same machines for their entire shift. They must understand their machines from a technical and functional aspect because fine tuning is often necessary. They typically have direct supervisors, but they are expected to handle everyday tasks without management assistance. Although not required, machinists should also understand the basics of electronics, pneumatics, and hydraulics.

Education and training

Schools offer training and certificates for machinists but the most common way to learn the critical aspects of the job is to work under the guidance of a journeyman. This learning is important for many reasons including the fact that machine parts are often manufactured to high tolerances that require expertise. Add to this the fact that these parts are sometimes produced in high volume, and it is relatively easy to see why training is important.

Example

Matilda works as a machinist at a plastics factory. Her job is to make lids for six-ounce and twelve-ounce plastic containers. Precision is necessary for this job because any lid with a tolerance exceeding .005 inches will not snap shut properly on the container. She produces about 8000 lids during her eight-hour shift, so mistakes could result in a lot of scrap material.

Matilda trained at her job for five years before she was allowed to make the lids without direct supervision, and now she has a skill that is very valuable to the plastics manufacturer. Her attention to detail is critical because it could affect the profitability of her organization, but she is trusted because she is an experienced machinist.

Carpentry

The following pertains to skilled tradespeople who are employed in manufacturing plants in a carpentry capacity:

Description

It is difficult to say how long carpentry has been around since people have worked with wood long before it was thought to be a trade. Their work went virtually unnoticed because it was considered a part of the process that led to the completion of projects, and most men had some type of woodworking skills in order to survive. However, over time, those woodworking skills evolved into a trade with its own recognition, commonly known today as carpentry.

Part of the evolution of carpentry is due to technological advances. Over the years, humans learned how to mass manufacture tools so workers doing carpentry work could focus on the jobs they were doing rather than creating the tools necessary to properly do those jobs. Today, computerized devices have made the planning, setup, and installation processes of jobs faster and more efficient; thereby allowing carpenters to take on multiple projects at the same time and finish them faster than they ever could do in the past.

In manufacturing operations, these skilled tradespeople set up and maintain building structures. The work with many different materials including metal, linoleum, marble, fiberglass, plastic, concrete, and wood, and they use those materials for flooring, framing, and creation of storage areas. Often times, they perform their work in virgin or untouched territory; thereby making them "pioneers" at their job sites. In other words, carpenters are typically the first tradespeople on the job, doing rough work that others will complete. They do not need to stay around until the job is finished, but those who are employed by manufacturers often check in periodically to see how the work is going and answer questions. This makes sense because their job often requires them to work in many different areas of the same plant so they are normally within walking distance of their completed projects.

In short, carpentry is a well-known trade that has evolved since its humble beginnings. Manufacturers understand the value of these tradespeople and utilized their knowledge and skills on a regular basis.

Education and training

Not surprisingly, training is required before carpenters are certified in their trade. This training involves book learning and on the job learning. First, aspiring carpenters take pre-apprentice courses in union approved college programs. After completing these programs, they begin their journey as apprentices under the watchful eyes of mentors who have practiced the trade and understand it well. After four or five years, they become journeymen, and further down the line they can take a test to become masters. Obviously, there is more involved with becoming a master carpenter than is shown in this paragraph, but it shows the basic steps involved.

Example

Bertram is a journeyman carpenter at a computer hardware assembling facility. He has been charged with the task of putting in a new marble floor in the foyer at the entrance of the plant offices. He uses a computer to map out how he will do the work and how many floor tiles will be needed to complete the project. After he knows what he needs to do and the number of floor tiles required, he purchases the tiles via an online supplier. The tiles are delivered to the plant, and Bertram begins installing them. After the installation, he leaves the job ready for the drywall people to do their work.

Tool & Die

The following pertains to skilled tradespeople who are employed in manufacturing plants in a tool and die capacity:

Description

Tool and die makers are unique tradespeople because they are usually only employed in manufacturing plants. They are machinists who make a variety of molds, dies, gauges and machine tools; most of which are used solely in production type operations.

Tool and die makers typically do not work in production areas. Instead, they are based out of machining shops or tool rooms so they have their own space, tools, and machinery to properly do their jobs. They can work alone or on teams that usually include engineers because engineers have many things in common with tool and die makers. For example, they both use math to resolve problems. Additionally, they both need a mechanical background in order to understand how machinery works. Last, but certainly not least, they both must have an understanding of science-based technology so they can apply the principles while trouble-shooting various manufacturing issues.

One major change tool and die tradespeople have undergone in recent years is they are now required to understand computer technology (it is no longer an option). For example, computer numerical control (CNC) is routinely referenced and utilized because it allows for the automation of machine tools via pre-programmed commands. This technological process is much faster, accurate, and efficient when compared to the wheels or levers that were hand-operated by employees in the past. Additionally, computer-aided design (CAD) allows for the creation, modification, and optimization of designs in a faster and more efficient manner.

In short, tool and die makers are needed in manufacturing, but they need to keep up with modern technology. Their worth is based on their ability to add value to production processes and, without technology, that value is limited.

Education and training

Most tool and die tradespeople undergo an apprentice under an experienced mentor. After about five years, they have enough experience to obtain the rank of journeyman and practice their trade without supervision. In other words, they are said to have mastered the necessary skills to properly do their jobs.

Interestingly, some tool and die makers graduate from accredited colleges and work thousands of hours to achieve journeyman status. This is by no means a shortcut, it is simply a way to become a tool and die tradesperson while earning a college degree.

Example

Donte is a tool and die maker employed at a small forklift assembly plant. One of his responsibilities involves designing dies for rollstock machinery that packages the paperwork and small parts that come with every forklift purchased by customers. Donte has a manufacturing engineer complete a computerized design of the dies along with the size and material requirements. He uses this design to create a 6-inch x 6-inch x 2-inch prototype using cast aluminum material. This prototype is tested on the rollstock machine by quality personnel and found to work properly. The prototype is returned to Donte and he creates three more identical dies (one for each rollstock pocket) for use by production employees.

Model making

Description

Model making tradespeople are assigned the responsibility of creating miniature representations of designs, ideas, and concepts. They create prototypes and mock-ups that can be critiqued before the actual construction or production begins. This critique is typically limited to the physical traits of the product or structure but it is also used for eye appeal; thereby making it valuable for sales and marketing personnel.

Model makers employed in manufacturing work in design shops, research facilities, and production areas. They need to know how to use a wide variety of equipment and machinery including lathes, saws, welders, and mills. Materials used include clay, wood, cement, metal, and plastic, and the overall process can get very detailed. These details include the finish and trim work because the end result needs to be representative of the product or structure designed for creation.

In short, model makers must have patience and the ability to pay attention to detail. Without these two traits, prototypes and mock-ups become rushed and the finished work does not appear professional. Professional appearance is important because, as with other jobs requiring manual labor, model makers are slowly being replaced by technological advances that are capable of saving money and time.

Education and training

As is the case with most trades, model makers need to go through some type of apprenticeship to achieve journeyman status. There is no specifically designed training program for this apprenticeship, but it should include practical design and model making. College coursework is typically not required even though it is available (although this requirement can vary depending on the employer). Quite simply, manufacturers prefer real-world experience over a certificate or degree. However, if the educational route is chosen, then creative courses, such as woodworking and ceramics, should be a major part of the curriculum along with model making and computer-aided design.

Example

Francine is a model maker for an architectural firm. She uses a blueprint developed by an architect to make a model of a building that will be used for visionary and structural purposes. The model is made out of brick and metal; thereby making it similar to the actual structure. After the building is created, it is critiqued by everyone at the firm involved in the building process, and modifications are made as deemed necessary. In the end, Francine's model is very representative of the real building, and it is approved by multiple people before any work is done on the actual structure.

Summary

Tradespeople are employed in manufacturing plants all over the world, and their contributions to the efficient operation of those plants cannot be underestimated. They work on processes ranging from simple to complex, and those processes produce the products necessary for organizational growth and prosperity.

This book explores skilled trades in manufacturing including electrical, plumbing, welding, heating and cooling, machinery, carpentry, tool & die, and model making. Each trade is described and the education and training necessary for certification or licensing are discussed. Examples are provided for further clarification, and the text is written for easy understanding at all reader levels.

Congratulations! You now understand more about skilled trades...essential jobs in every manufacturing facility.

Lawyers
Short and Simple Explanation Series
Book 4

Louis Bevoc

Published by
NutriNiche System LLC

Louis Bevoc books...simple explanations of complex subjects

Introduction

This is the fourth book in a series of short and simple explanations of professions. For every book, the profession is described along with a discussion on the required education and training. These books are written so people can inform and educate themselves on various professions without having to understand difficult language or complex terminology…which is the underlying philosophy of all Louis Bevoc books.

In today's world, lawsuits take precedence over just about anything. People are so inclined to sue others that they take legal action when something appears wrong or things do not go their way. Quite simply, they want some type of compensation the alleged pain and suffering that they have endured, and they are willing to do whatever is legally necessary to get that compensation. The large number of lawsuits that occur today might be unfortunate, but they are real and will not likely be reduced anytime in the near future.

Lawsuits stem from race, religion, health, business, money, death, crime, injury, and work; thereby making the legal services of lawyers more important now than they have ever been in the past. Professional lawyers, also known as attorneys, serve as advocates for people who are the initiators or recipients of lawsuits or other legal matters such as eviction notices, cease & desist orders, court summons, parole violations, and other matters where legal documents have been issued.

Legal services are so popular today that over 100,000 students are enrolled in law schools all over the world. These students are tempted by the money, power, and prestige associated with the affluent attorney lifestyle. However, the supply of lawyers today exceeds the demand; thereby resulting in some law school graduates finding themselves without jobs. These graduates are qualified to do legal work in some capacity, but their services are simply not needed or worth the expense.

Working lawyers have a variety of job responsibilities including (1) solving problems with laws, regulations, and legal theories, (2) acting as counselors for legal advice, (3) acting as spokespersons or advocates for an individuals, groups, or organizations, and (4) providing defense or prosecution representation for lawsuits. The combination of these responsibilities is overwhelming and nearly impossible for one lawyer to handle, and that is why attorneys focus on specialized aspects of the law. These specializations, also known as types, are the premise of this book. Each type is described and discussed using terminology that average people are easily able to understand.

Now that you have a basic understanding of lawyers and the basis of this book, let's move forward. The next section explores the common specializations of law that are the focus of lawyers' practices. These specializations can be debated or sub-divided into further categories, but they provide a basic understanding of what lawyers do and what is required for them to achieve their legal status. Please keep in mind that some attorney responsibilities overlap; thereby making it difficult to completely segregate the specializations.

Types

The following are unique specializations of lawyers practicing in the United States and other areas of the world:

Description

These attorneys are typically used when the liabilities of people or businesses heavily outweigh their assets and they choose to go bankrupt rather than struggle to pay off their debts. Bankruptcy is not the ideal situation, but it is the best choice when all efforts to rectify financial situations are unsuccessful. In some ways, people are happy to see bankruptcy lawyers because these professionals work toward removing the stress and anxiety associated with debt.

Bankruptcy lawyers handle business and personal bankruptcy proceedings from start to finish. The offer legal advice on what their clients need to do to successfully declare bankruptcy, and they also fill out the necessary paperwork. This paperwork is quite complex and cumbersome, and it usually requires an experienced professional to properly complete it. However, in order to complete the paperwork, bankruptcy lawyers require their clients to provide a variety of different documents. These documents include tax returns, real estate transactions, income statements (from banks, mutual funds, stocks, retirement, alimony, child support, etc.), and any other assets that reduce liabilities such as vehicles, collections, and intellectual works.

Bankruptcy attorneys also provide their clients with information regarding credit counseling. This is important because, since 2005, United States law dictates that people must take a credit counseling course before filing for bankruptcy. Some people are exempt from this law, but the majority of people need to follow it regardless of the obviousness of the situation. Bankruptcy attorneys let their clients know if they are exempt or, if applicable, the steps they can take to achieve the exempt status.

Essentially, the required credit counseling course prepares individualized budgets for people that suggest options for paying back debt. People do not have to follow the suggestions, but they need to include them in their paperwork if they decide to file for bankruptcy. Once they have filed, US law dictates that they must take another course in debtor education. As most bankrupt attorneys will advise, the debtor education course has some value because it shows how to rebuild credit after bankruptcy. If the two required courses are not completed, then the bankruptcy case is thrown out of court and the filer has to start the process all over again.

On an interesting note, bankruptcy attorneys are unique because they have the ability to create very ironic situations if their law firm declares bankruptcy. This might seem something that would never happen, but it has occurred and many people (usually clients) are negatively affected. These people go from a bad situation to a situation that is worse; thereby making it more difficult for their financial survival.

Training and Education

Aspiring bankruptcy lawyers must first obtain an undergraduate degree. This degree is not specified, but most students who plan to become attorneys graduate with a political science, history, sociology, or economics degree. However, law schools consider grade point averages important for the selection process, so students should choose a major where they receive good grades. For example, students who struggle with accounting and statistics should probably not choose finance as their major.

After graduation, aspiring bankruptcy attorneys need to take the Law School Admission Test (LSAT) to be considered for law school. Accredited law schools do not accept students who have not taken this test; thereby making it absolutely essential. Similar to grade point averages, high LSAT scores are critical for admission, even though life experience is taken into consideration.

Once students are in law schools, the countdown to their Juris Doctor begins…as long as they do not drop out or get expelled from the program. Many different courses are taken and they are often related to civil proceedings, wrongful acts, regulations, and general laws. Students who want to specialize in bankruptcy are strongly encouraged to take courses geared toward personal and business bankruptcy laws and procedures.

After earning their Juris Doctor (JD) degrees, prospective bankruptcy attorneys need to pass the bar exam for the state where they intend to practice. This exam is quite detailed and cumbersome, and there is no guarantee of passing it. It takes hours of preparation time and encompasses many situations that lawyers encounter, but individuals who pass this exam indicate they are ready to start working as attorneys.

After bankruptcy lawyers pass the bar exam, they need to undergo additional training. This training takes place in law firms that specialize in personal or business bankruptcy under the watchful eyes of experienced attorneys. Sometimes this training is conducted during an internship, but other times it occurs when the new graduates find employment with bankruptcy law firms for the purpose of gaining experience and networking for future jobs. After the training is completed, attorneys are considered specialists in the area of bankruptcy and promote themselves as such to potential clients.

Note: For simplifications purposes and to avoid repeating the same wording, the steps of (1) obtaining an undergraduate degree, (2) completing the LSAT, and (3) completing law school, and (4) passing the bar exam will be referred to as *normal education requirements for lawyers* for the remainder of the attorney specializations.

Intellectual property

Description

These lawyers are possibly the most interesting type of attorneys because they work to protect things that cannot be depleted and are typically not visible. Intellectual property is not a product or a service, it is an intangible creation of the mind. It includes trade secrets, trademarks, licensing, artistic works, brands, patents, inventions, copyrights, ideas, compositions, designs, symbols, and phrases.

Intellectual property lawyers defend and protect people's and organizations' rights to their intellectual creations. They advise clients that this protection of intellect is not forever, but, while it is protected, others cannot use it without express permission. This window of protection allows the clients to profit from their intellectual property without the fear that others will do so by copying or stealing. It also encourages people to create because they know they will be rewarded for their efforts if those efforts are well received by the masses.

Intellectual property lawyers play a critical role for their clients because those clients cannot provide protection for their intellectual property like they can for their physical property. For example, people who want to stop others from stealing their chickens' eggs can put up chicken wire. However, there is no wire that can be put up for intellectual property because physical boundaries do not exist…which is why intellectual property attorneys are of great value to their clients.

Many times, intellectual property is the most valuable asset of an organization. This might seem strange because it is an intangible asset, but it is true due to perception. For example, the brand of Coca-Cola is well-known all over the world. Any item with the Coke logo, regardless of whether or not it is soda, is instantly recognized; thereby increasing the value of that item. Coca-Cola's intellectual property has a value that is much greater than the company's physical inventory. In fact, the value of this brand is so high that it is difficult to place a monetary value on it.

Without intellectual property lawyers, businesses and individuals have a difficult time holding on to intangible assets that they create and own. Since laws are always broken by unscrupulous individuals looking for opportunities to cash in on other people's hard work, these attorneys' skills will always be needed.

Training and education

First, aspiring intellectual property attorneys need to complete the *normal education requirements for lawyers.* Courses in law school should be geared toward laws regarding copyrights, patents, and licensing. In today's legal world, it is also important to understand laws related to the internet and cyberspace.

After passing the bar exam, lawyers who want to specialize in intellectual property should take one more exam issued by the United States Patent and Trademark Office (USPTO). Attorneys who pass this exam are listed on the register of the UPSTO; thereby allowing them to interact with UPSTO officials…which is very important for their careers.

Once the UPSTO exam is successfully completed, lawyers are ready to enter the work world of intellectual property law while promoting themselves as qualified. As they work, they learn from more experienced attorneys and gradually build a clientele that they can use for furthering their careers.

Personal injury

Description

These lawyers are sometimes the highest paid and most well-known specialization because their cases can make people a lot of money. Essentially, personal injury attorneys help people get compensated for mental or physical injury that allegedly resulted from encounters with a person or an organization. Their goal is to find the defendant guilty so their clients can collect money for their misfortune and they can get paid a percentage of that money in return for their services. In this role, personal injury attorneys act as prosecutors. However, these professionals also act as defense lawyers for people or organizations that are being sued because they understand the laws pertaining to defendants and plaintiffs.

Lawsuits involving personal injury often stem from mental or physical injuries received from slander, accidents, ineffective services, or defective products. These injuries can be sustained at home, work, or a public place…but the common denominator is someone or something is responsible and needs to pay for their wrongdoing.

Often referred to as trial lawyers, personal injury attorneys are unique because they spend most of their time researching how they are going to argue in court. They interview people, create documents, depose witnesses, research laws, and determine monetary compensation for their clients. Not surprisingly, they need to travel to different locations to properly do their jobs. This travel can be local, national, or international depending on what or who is involved with the case. However, clients pay for that travel, and the costs can be staggering.

Like it or not, the world has more lawsuits today than have ever occurred in the past. This trend does not appear to be slowing down because the financial payoffs can be substantial. This is bad for the people or organizations getting sued, but it is good for people doing the suing and the lawyers who represent them.

Training and education

First, aspiring personal injury attorneys need to complete the *normal education requirements for lawyers*. Courses in law school should be geared toward analytical reasoning, health law, advocacy, problem-solving, and negotiation. These attorneys do a great deal of research, so the problem-solving courses should require "digging deep" into the related subject matter in order to come up with the best possible solution.

After passing the bar exam, personal injury lawyers are technically qualified to practice. The word "technically" is important because further training and education help these new attorneys become better in their specialization. Some states offer certification for personal injury lawyers who spend a lot of time in trials. Additionally, some universities offer graduate degrees in law that focus on advocacy and health law. The programs for these degrees often include internships where attorneys gain real-world experience under knowledgeable professionals.

Experienced personal injury lawyers have a variety of different job opportunities that they can explore. They can own or work for an independent practice, which has the potential to be very financially lucrative, or they can work for insurance companies as liability specialists. Another job option is to work for organizations that require legal expertise for lawsuits or other problems brought about by consumers, employees, government agencies, watchdog groups, and the general public. However, regardless of the direction they take for employment, most personal liability lawyers need to excel during trials in order to properly do their jobs.

Estate

Description

The main job of estate layers is to plan for people after they are deceased. This involves drafting their clients' wills (and forms of wills known as living trusts) to ensure those clients final wishes are adhered to and will withstand legal protests. Wills are important, especially for those who are wealthy, because they document the distribution of assets. Estate attorneys have a very good understanding of estate laws and they know what needs to be documented to make sure assets end up in the hands of the people designated to receive them

Unfortunately, estate lawyers are sometimes the lowest paid type of attorneys because their services are not typically considered an immediate need. Most people are not in a hurry to prepare their wills for a few reasons, some of which are as follows:

- The preparation of wills forces people to think about their mortality. Most individuals want to avoid this thought because death is a difficult subject to envision due to the fear of the unknown.
- There are many laws already in place that cannot be changed without the consent of those excluded from wills. For example, certain laws require legal spouses to sign off on wills that exclude them from being the beneficiaries.
- Wills can be expensive and require a lot of time and effort. The cost and effort can be outrageous if the will is a living trust that is constantly being changed...which is not uncommon for people with a lot of money.

However, regardless of the reasons that prevent people from establishing wills, there will always be a need for estate attorneys because there are always people who want to have their affairs in line at the time of their deaths.

Experienced estate attorneys have career options because they have a good understanding of family law, estate law, and taxation law. Armed with this knowledge, they can work in estate planning firms, financial planning companies, banks, accounting firms, or law firms. Their opportunities within these organizations are wide open if they choose the management route; thereby providing them with job diversity that might not be as accessible for other lawyer specialists.

Education and training

First, aspiring estate attorneys need to complete the *normal education requirements for lawyers.* Their law school courses should focus on estate law and taxation, but they might also want to explore a sub-specialization in family law or real estate law which wil help them establish a niche in their profession.

After passing the bar exam, estate lawyers are technically qualified to practice, but many of them accept internships for real-world experience. Estate lawyers can also benefit from formal post-law school education in the form of a master's degree that hones their professional skills.

Immigration

Description

The spotlight on immigration all over the world has resulted in immigration lawyers becoming more in demand today than they have ever been in the past. In the United States, these attorneys work on virtually every aspect of immigration, regardless of whether that immigration is legal or illegal. Specifically, they represent immigrants who are citizens, applying for citizenship, illegal residents, or refugees.

Many immigrants are limited in terms of monetary resources, especially if they are refugees from war-torn nations, so some immigration attorneys work as humanitarians with little or no pay. In this charitable role, these lawyers often fight for basic human rights and defend their clients against the violation of those rights including deportation issues. However, wealthy foreigners also immigrate to the United States and are threatened with being deported, and those individuals pay handsomely for their citizenship. The compensations balance between affluent and poor clients allows immigrations attorneys the opportunity to earn a good living.

Immigration attorneys work in private and public settings, and they are expected to grow in numbers due to their ever-increasing need. Unlike some other lawyer specialists, these attorneys typically do not venture into alternative fields to practice professionally, but finding work in immigration is typically not a problem.

Training and education

Like every other lawyer, aspiring immigration attorneys must first complete the *normal education requirements for lawyers.* Their law school courses should revolve around immigration law and naturalization law. Other more specific coursework can focus on laws related to political asylum and refugee status.

One factor that differentiates immigration attorneys from many other lawyer specialists is the law clinics that are available in many law schools. These clinics focus on the laws of immigration and allow students to work with actual immigrants and refugees in order to gain experience. Work done out in the field is discussed in classrooms, and the overall learning experience is much better than classroom work alone.

Criminal defense

Description

Criminal defense attorneys represent people who have been accused of some type of legal wrongdoing or misconduct. They spend their time researching the best methods for defending these people against their charges. This research entails travel to witnesses, experts, prisons, courtrooms, law libraries, and just about anywhere else they need to go to collect evidence that defends their clients. When on a case that goes to trial, defense attorneys often work in excess of 70 hours in order to do the job necessary to win the case. Their goal is to have their clients found not guilty so those clients can walk away as free people.

A major skill required for defense attorneys is the ability to constructively argue. They need to build cases and convince jurors that there is reasonable doubt that their clients are guilty of the crimes they are accused of committing. Their arguing process needs to be methodical and well-planned. Information must be given to the jurors at the right time…not all in the beginning or at the end, which is why argumentative skills are so important.

One challenging aspect of being a defense attorney involves ethics. These lawyers sometimes represent people that they believe are guilty of the crimes they are accused of committing, but, as defense attorneys, they must work their hardest to achieve a not guilty verdict. This can pose a very ethical dilemma…especially if there are victims and families of victims who have suffered because of the crime.

Experienced criminal defense attorneys are paid well for their services. Typically they charge some type of retainer fee, but they can also be hired on an hourly pay basis. If they are skilled, defense attorneys rarely look at other fields to practice their profession. They understand how to defend those who are accused, and they make a good living doing it.

Training and education

Aspiring criminal defense attorneys must first complete the *normal education requirements for lawyers.* Courses in law school should be geared toward argumentative strategy, persuasion, and research. Other coursework might involve negotiation and problem solving, but the main focus should be on methodical arguing in a persuasive manner.

In addition to the bar exam, criminal attorneys must pass a test on ethics. This test is important because, as noted earlier in this section, these lawyers' jobs can pose ethical dilemmas. In short, it is understood by everyone associated with legal services that defense attorneys risk behaving in ways that are unethical when defending their clients.

After the ethics exam, these lawyers are ready to work in their field as professionals. It often takes time for them to build their reputations as being good defense attorneys, but they gradually build a clientele that is used to further their careers.

Prosecuting

Description

These lawyers typically represent the government in court cases involving criminals. Their job, which is the exact opposite of criminal defense attorneys, is to get juries to convict people of their accused crimes. Similar to defense lawyers, prosecuting attorneys need to methodically argue their cases in order to persuade people on juries to find people guilty beyond a reasonable doubt.

Prosecuting attorneys need research skills in order to properly do their jobs. They interview witnesses, talk to victims, review police reports, and gather any type of information that can be used against defendants. They also work with government officials, law enforcement personnel, and experts because these individuals provide valuable insight and are considered credible witnesses when put on the stand to testify.

Prosecuting attorneys often use their skills to play on the emotions of jury members. If they can get those members to be sympathetic toward the pain and suffering of the victims, then they have a better chance of winning the case. In fact, some people's emotions control their behavior so strongly that they vote to convict even if they have reasonable doubt. This might not be right, but it does happen and astute prosecuting attorneys use it to their advantage.

Prosecutors are unique attorneys because they have to communicate with all parties involved in the case including the defense. They are required by law to disclose all evidence pertaining to the case so the defense can use it to their benefit. In other words, prosecuting lawyers must provide evidence that might exonerate the people they are prosecuting. This appears quite contradictory, but it is the law.

Skilled prosecuting attorneys have a wealth of knowledge about the internal workings of government and law enforcement agencies, and that knowledge is very beneficial for many clients. These lawyers are usually employed by the local, state, or federal governments and their jobs are to convict people for the crimes they are accused of committing. However, their argumentative skills are valuable and sought after by a wide variety of legal professionals, so private law firms also hire them. In fact, many prosecuting attorneys go into private practice at some point in their career due to the opportunity for higher earnings.

Training and education

Aspiring prosecuting attorneys need to first complete the *normal education requirements for lawyers.* Courses in law school should be geared toward argumentative strategy, criminal law, and research. Other coursework might involve public speaking and rhetoric, but, similar to a defense attorney's education, the main focus should be on argument and persuasion.

After the bar exam, prosecuting attorneys can begin to practice. If they work for a government agency, then they will most likely have mentors that show them the best ways to do their job. This process allows them to learn as they move forward with their careers, similar to an internship with full-time pay and benefits.

Family

Description

Family lawyers deal with issues pertaining to families, including those that occur in family businesses. They are probably best known for handling cases involving child custody, guardianship, paternity, and juvenile delinquency. Their cases can be psychologically draining because people are fighting with their own flesh and blood and emotions run high, so they need to be prepared for the fallout that might transpire.

Family lawyers face challenges that are unique when compared to other attorneys. These challenges stem from the close relationships between family members that can lead to conflict. Conflict is not bad if it is functional, but dysfunctional conflict results in people being attacked instead of problems; thereby adding another dimension to establishing peace and getting family members to work together. Based on the unique nature of their clientele, family lawyers need to be skilled in psychological understanding, social awareness, and conflict resolution in order to do their jobs to the best of their abilities.

Some responsibilities of family attorneys overlap with estate lawyers, but a family lawyer's entire focus is the family while the family is only one part of an estate attorney's job function. Additionally, some responsibilities of family attorneys overlap with those of immigration lawyers, but family lawyers are not restricted to immigrant families. However, regardless of common ground shared with other attorneys, family lawyers provide a needed service due to their specialized knowledge.

Family attorneys often work in private firms, educational facilities, and government agencies because these environments require their professional skills. However, they are also valuable to other types of law-based organizations because they deal with a wide variety of legal issues when representing entire families or individual family members.

Training and education

As expected, aspiring family attorneys need to first complete the *normal education requirements for lawyers.* Courses in law school should be geared toward communication, psychology, conflict resolution. Other areas of study might include emotional intelligence and social work, but the key is to understand human behavior.

Similar to the education available to immigration attorneys, some law schools offer family law clinics where students can gain real-world experience under the watchful eyes of mentors. These clinics function like co-ops because students bring their experiences back to their classrooms for discussion.

After passing the bar exam, most family lawyers are allowed to practice. However, some states require these professionals to become certified in the field of family law before they are formally recognized as family attorneys.

Summary

Lawyers represent people and organizations in a wide variety of environments and situations. It is sometimes difficult to estimate the value of these professionals because some people find them beneficial while others find them a hindrance. However, it can be said with confidence that attorneys will be around as long as laws are broken or people have disagreements.

This book focuses on the legal profession. Specifically, it examines lawyers and their specializations including bankruptcy law, intellectual property law, personal injury law, estate law, immigration law, criminal defense law, prosecution law, and family law. Each specialization is described and the necessary education and training are discussed. The text is informational and educational, and it is written for easy understanding at all reader levels.

Congratulations! You know more about specialized lawyers...essential professionals for people and organizations all over the world.

Nurses

Short and Simple Explanation Series
Book 5

Louis Bevoc

Published by
NutriNiche System LLC

Louis Bevoc books...simple explanations of complex subjects

Introduction

This is the fifth book in a series of short and simple explanations of professions. For every book, the profession is described along with a discussion on the required education and training. These books are written so people can inform and educate themselves on various professions without having to understand difficult language or complex terminology...which is the underlying philosophy of all Louis Bevoc books.

In one form or another, nurses have been around for thousands of years. They started out as people who understood a little about anatomy and were able to determine when others were in need of medical care. Primitive as it may have been, their observations and recommendations were based on knowledge they accrued during their lives and "patients" were, at the very least, made more comfortable when sick, injured, or diseased.

The nurses of long ago did their best to help people in need, but their practices were elementary and mostly based on beliefs and ideas rather than hard facts. The first nursing "professionals" stemmed from people in religious organizations who were intent on helping others in the community. They made themselves available for those in need and used science-based thinking for diagnosis and treatment. For example, they might have noticed that more people get sick from certain types of plants or skin heals best if it covered after being torn or cut. These nurses were nowhere near as knowledgeable, educated, and trained as today's medical professionals, but they started pushing nursing down the path it would follow into the future.

Florence Nightingale is probably the first person who was truly thought of as a nurse, and she provided the foundation for the nursing practices of today. Ms. Nightingale was a social reformer who realized the importance of sanitary standards. She applied her ideas to injured and sick soldiers during the Crimean War and, based on her success, went on to establish the first nursing school in the world. Specifically, Nightingale believed poor living conditions, especially those related to sanitation, increased the death rate of soldiers injured in battle. She specified fresh air and fresh water as being essential for good sanitation, and she was able to reduce soldier death rates in the war by making sure both of these resources were in supply using a staff of women who functioned as nurses.

There is a lot more to Florence Nightingale than can be discussed in the scope of this book, but the main point of her story is to show how she important she was to the field of nursing. Although some historians debate the success of her war efforts, nobody denies that she was a pioneer in the development of nursing as a profession.

The history of nursing is an interesting topic, but this book focuses on nursing that occurs today. Nurses are trained professionals who concentrate on the care, healing, and overall health of their patients. Traditionally, they work under the supervision of medical doctors, but their roles have evolved and become much more complex since World War II. They now have various levels of authority depending on their education, training, experience, position, and employer.

Many nurses work independently due to the specialized training and certifications that they have received. Nurse practitioners, for example, are now allowed by law to set up their own practices. Their function similar to a physician's assistant (PA), but they do not have to answer to a doctor. They are in charge, and they diagnose and treat as based on their observations and knowledge.

Today's nurses are routinely responsible for coordinating patient care plans that utilize teams of medical professionals. These teams are developed based on specific patient needs and can include medical doctors, psychiatrists, psychologists, therapists, social workers, and other nurses. Coordinating nurses work with people on the team to diagnose and treat health-related problems. In some cases, the coordinating nurses diagnose and treat patients without the aid of other team members...something that they could not do in the not-so-distant past.

Like it or not, people often associate nurses with hospitals. Yes, nurses are in hospitals, but they also work in other types of settings including clinics, doctor's offices, humanitarian organizations, nursing homes, schools, military bases, government agencies, rehab centers, and home health care companies. Some nurses are self-employed, serving as personal health professionals for individuals in need of medical assistance.

An interesting fact about nursing is that it is female dominated. It is considered a skilled and well-paying career choice, but men tend to shy away from it. This avoidance might be based on the false perception of nurses as caregivers rather than medical professionals. Caregiving is part of a nurse's job, but it is much less significant now than it was in the past. Nurses, just like doctors, focus on the practice of medicine, health care, and the healing process.

Now that you have a basic understanding of the nursing profession, let's move forward to the next section that explores common specializations of nurses. Please note that these specializations can be added to or sub-divided into further categories, but they provide a basic understanding of what nurses do and what is required for them to achieve their positions. Also, keep in mind that some nurses' responsibilities overlap; thereby making it difficult to completely segregate the specializations.

Types

Licensed practical nurse (LPN)

Description

Licensed practical nurses (LPN) are the most basic type of nurse and, as such, require less formal education and training than other nurse specialists. The typically work under the supervision of a registered nurse (RN); thereby performing many of the same duties without having the responsibility of assuring that every task is completed and all employees under the RN's supervision are doing what they are supposed to be doing. In other words, LPNs are typically not employed in management roles.

It is important to understand that each state determines the jobs that LPNs can perform, and individual companies also assign differing jobs. However, in general, specific job tasks of LPNs include dressing wounds, collecting urine samples, drawing blood, and taking temperatures and blood pressure (also known as vitals). They also do some clerical work and can be assigned to a desk when the need arises.

LPNs are typically not allowed to develop treatment plans for patients. They can gather information regarding patients' health, but they cannot analyze or evaluate that information in order to make a diagnosis. Supervising RNs usually analyze the information and treat the problem under the watchful eyes of a physician.   This protocol is subject to change, but it provides a basic understanding of what LPNs can and cannot do on the job.

Education and training

A high school diploma, or its equivalent, along with a minimum grade point average (GPA) is usually required to be admitted to most LPN programs. Additionally, prerequisite courses in science, statistics, and English are also required before aspiring LPNs are admitted.   GPA is also a factor in the prerequisite programs and a C is usually the minimum grade that is considered acceptable.

Another requirement for acceptance into an LPN program is a passing grade on the entrance exam. This exam is known as the Test of Essential Academic Skills (TEAS), and it contains four different sections of questions on reading, science, math, English. Essentially, these questions determine whether a student has the ability to handle the LPN program.

LPN programs usually focus on science, nursing, pharmacology, and pathology courses along with a required clinical internship for practical experience. Some LPN programs require the completion of a certified nurse aide (CNA) program. The CNA program takes 6-12 months to complete (depending on part-time or full-time status) and requires students to pass a final examination.   CNAs are a great way to learn the job functions of nurses in the real world because students are required to spend time with patients performing nursing tasks.

While in the LPN program, aspiring licensed practical nurses need to choose between a certificate and an associate degree. This selection is important because the certificate is designed to be terminal (no further education is desired) while the associate degree is designed for continuation into a registered nurse (RN) program. Not surprisingly, the associate degree takes longer to complete than the certificate, and it requires more clinical work. However, regardless of the path taken, LPN programs produce licensed practical nurses with the necessary skills and credentials to practice in their chosen profession.

Regardless of the coursework path chosen, LPNs need to pass a test before they are licensed to practice. This test is known as the National Council Licensure Examination - Practical Nursing (NCLEX-PN), and it is issued by the National Council of State Boards of Nursing. It includes sections on medication, patient care, and general nursing. Nurses must also be certified in CPR, but this is usually achieved during school.

Registered nurse (RN)

Description

A registered nurse (RN) is a step above and licensed practical nurse and that is why RNs typically supervise LPNs. RNs are required to meet the needs of their patients in terms of medical care and comfort. They are on the front line of hospitals, often acting as a gateway to the physicians that are their bosses.

RNs must have the ability to solve problems and think critically because they sometimes need to develop care plans based on their analysis and diagnoses of their patients. In this role, they function similar to a physician as they determine what is best for the individual needs of their patients.

RNs are most commonly employed in hospitals. Some are floor nurses who go from room to room handling the needs of a variety of different patients while others specialize in designated areas such as emergency rooms, surgery rooms, or offices (as managers). It is not uncommon for these nurses to perform many different jobs in the course of their careers. For example, some RNs start out assisting surgeons during operations, then move to floor nurse positions, and finish their careers as managers who oversee other employees.

RNs who do not work in hospitals typically find employment in doctor's offices, rehab centers, aging facilities, prisons, government agencies, home health care companies, and the military. This list of employment opportunities is extensive due to the diverse skills offered by RNs. In these roles, they typically take on a variety of tasks rather than specialize in one or two due to the limited resources of their employers. Hospitals can employ many different types of nurses, while smaller private firms typically do not have that option due to financial restrictions.

Education and training

As mentioned in the LPN section, RNs can be LPNs who chose to continue their education. However, they can also start out on a path that directly leads to RN status. Regardless of the path chosen, aspiring RNs need to obtain an associate's degree or bachelor's degree from an accredited nursing school before they are allowed to take the National Council Licensure Examination - Practical Nursing (NCLEX-PN) issued by the National Council of State Boards of Nursing NCLEX-RN. After they pass this exam, they can obtain their license to practice.

RNs who choose the minimum education of an associate's degree (ASN) typically take courses in science and medical terminology. They also undergo some type of training in medical settings, often hospitals. RNs who earn their bachelor's degree (BSN) receive a broader educational experience due to their elective courses, but, more importantly, they have the opportunity to specialize in areas of nursing such as mental health or surgery.

RNs can also earn master's degrees (MSN) if they want more education and the benefits that go with it. Nurses who obtain a master's degree often move into supervisory roles, teach, or become practitioners. The curriculum for the MSN program is theory driven in terms or research, leadership, and change in the field of nursing. Not surprising, nurses with Master's degrees usually receive higher pay than those with less education.

Regardless of the degree obtained, RNs must pass the NCLEX-RN exam. Similar to the Practical Nursing (NCLEX-PN) discussed in the LPN section, this exam includes sections on medication, patient care, and general nursing. However, the test for RNs is more complex and covers more diverse subject matter.

Pediatric nurse

Description

Pediatric nurses are RNS who perform a wide variety of nursing functions such as drawing book, collecting urine, administering immunizations, and measuring vitals. However, their main job is to serve the medical needs of children from infancy to adolescence, and sometimes after adolescence depending on the circumstances. They work with pediatricians or other physicians in hospitals or other medical settings, but they can also do casework for the government or private companies. Pediatric nurses' jobs involve determining medical problems of kids and recommending plans of action for the restoration of their health prevention of reoccurrences.

In addition to their medical skills, pediatric nurses must have patience and understanding. Kids do not always provide accurate answers to questions; thereby making it challenging to accurately diagnose their problems. Additionally, children do not behave like adults, and they can present special problems when being treated. They might scream as if they are in agonizing pain, even though the only pain they actually feel is from the needle of a syringe. Pediatric nurses must be able to handle this type of behavior without emotionally charged reactions.

Another job aspect that sets pediatric nurses apart from other RNs is that they must deal with the legal guardians of children who are under their care. They spend a good deal of time informing and educating parents about the diseases or illnesses of their children. They discuss the causes of problems, treatment plans, and preventative measures to avoid reoccurrences.   This is particularly important for parents whose children have special needs such as cancer or juvenile diabetes.

The last unique part of pediatric nurses' jobs is their travel. They often go to schools, neighborhood gatherings, concerts, and fairs to provide health-related information and services. In this role, they educate a broad base of children and parents on the diagnosis, treatment, and prevention of childhood injuries, illnesses, and diseases. Fortunately, they usually advise parents who are interested in learning because they place a high value on their children, but that interest does not guarantee the parents will follow through with what they have learned after once they are home and back in a normal routine.

Education and training

Nurses who aspire to achieve pediatric status must first become RNs. This process is described under the *education and training* part of the *Registered Nurse (RN)* section in this book. Courses taken to achieve an RN status, such as general nursing and medical terminology, are similar to those required for other RNs However pediatric nurses also take courses in child psychology and child development to better prepare themselves for their careers.

In addition to a college degree, RNs can obtain certificates for pediatric nursing after passing exams. They can also continue their education in master's programs that lead to them becoming nurse practitioners (NP). NPs can do many things that physicians do such as prescribing medication and designing healthcare plans.

Oncology nurse

Description

Oncology nurses are typically not as well-known as RNs to the average person because their jobs are specialized and limited to a relativity small portion of the population. However, their jobs are highly visible and very important to the patients they treat because those patients are affected by cancer. In fact, many cancer survivors remember their oncology nurses better than they remember the oncology physicians who supervised their care.

Oncology nurses monitor their patients' physical health while administering antibiotics and chemotherapy for blood-related matters as deemed necessary. Since the doses of chemo medications need to be exact, these nurses need to be detail oriented. They must also be compassionate when working with patients and the families and friends of those patients. This compassion requires them to have the ability to control their emotions due to the potential of their patients' health worsening...even to the point of death.

Oncology nurses do some travel, but their jobs are mostly based in cancer care settings such as medical clinics and hospitals. They are different from other nurses because they experience very happy and very depressing situations. When people beat cancer, everyone is joyful and elated...but when they lose the battle and die, everyone is sad and deflated. Since they are involved in life and death situations on a daily basis, and it is relatively easy to understand why oncology nurses are unique.

Education and training

Aspiring oncology nurses need to first become RNs. This process is described under the *education and training* part of the *Registered Nurse (RN)* section in this book. Their college coursework typically involves physiology and anatomy in addition to the general nursing requirements.   They can also obtain master's degrees in programs that focus specifically on oncology-related aspects of nursing such as cancer detection, pharmacology, and hospice care.

Oncology nurses must obtain certifications in order to perform certain job functions. For example, they need to chemo certification to administer chemotherapy drugs and develop treatment plans. They become certified oncology nurses after completing programs offered by authorized institutions.

Intensive care nurse

Description

Intensive care nurses, also known as critical care nurses, are RNs who focus on patients in hospital intensive care units. These patients typically have serious, life-threatening illnesses or injuries that require specialized nursing skills before, during, and after medical treatment. Common treatment involves surgery after some type of trauma or accident, and that surgery is usually invasive and risky.

Due to the nature of their jobs, intensive care nurses almost always have fewer patients under their care. Their complete attention is needed when determining medication doses, using ventilators, and providing care for patients whose lives are at risk if wrong decisions are made.

As is the case for most nurses, intensive care nurses are always in demand. However, intensive nurse care is especially needed because the number of people in intensive care units is steadily rising. In fact, intensive care is so popular today that it has been suggested that intensive care nurses be further divided into infant, children, and adult specializations....but this division has not yet formally taken place.

Regardless of the fact that the intensive care nurse profession has not been "officially" divided into subcategories, there is a form of this specialization that does exist. Intensive care units (ICU) are often divided into cardiac, burn, neurological, and other types of units so specialized care can be provided. In these units, intensive care nurses assume the roles of specialists while working with physicians who assume the same roles; thereby creating informal subdivisions of the intensive care nursing profession.

Education and training

People who want to become intensive care nurses must first achieve RN status. This process is described under the *education and training* part of the *Registered Nurse (RN)* section in this book. Courses taken include anatomy, life-threatening illnesses, and serious injuries in addition to the required RN coursework.

Once they become RNs, aspiring intensive care units need to gain at least one year of experience in other nursing positions, such as surgical operations, before being considered for intensive care jobs. They also need additional training in cardiac life support so they can treat cardiac arrest and other serious medical situations.

After becoming intensive care nurses, these professionals have a longer orientation period than other nurse specialists due to the need for a detailed understanding of their job functions.

Operating room nurse

These professionals' skills are needed for surgical procedures, and their presence can be life-saving. Similar to oncology nurses, they care for patients before and after surgery. Also, similar to oncology nurses, they deal with the patients' friends and family members in situations that can be rather difficult. However, unlike oncology nurses, operation room nurses focus is not limited to cancer; thereby requiring them to have a broader range of skills and knowledge.

Job responsibilities of operating room nurses include getting patients ready for surgery, assisting surgeons, and servicing patients' medical needs during the recovery and healing processes. In addition to sterilizing surgical tools and distributing those tools to surgeons, they assist with medical issues as needed during operations. Examples include helping doctors control bleeding, regulate breathing, or suture wounds of patients.

The best operating room nurses are fast learners who adapt to change in environments that can undergo change on a moment's notice. They work in stressful situations so they also need to be able to work under pressure. In short, intelligence and composure are important traits for these professionals.

Education and training

As noted for every specialization in this book, people who want to become operating room nurses must first achieve RN status. This process is described under the *education and training* part of the *Registered Nurse (RN)* section discussed earlier. The required RN core coursework needs to be completed, but aspiring operating room nurses should also take courses in operating room procedures, anesthesia protocols, and surgical tool understanding.

Once practicing, RNs are often required to obtain operating room nursing certificates before they are allowed to become operating room nurses. These certificates typically require study and experience in order to take and pass a required examination. It should also be noted that the certification is only good for a limited time period, and re-certification is necessary upon expiration.

Anesthesia nurse

Description

Anesthesia nurses, commonly known as nurse anesthetists, require more education, training, and certification than most of the other nurse specializations discussed in this book. This is due to the fact that they administer anesthetics and other medications in addition to monitoring the vital signs of the patients under their care. Mistakes can be fatal, so complete understanding of situations is critical.

Nurse anesthetists usually work in hospitals where surgical operations are performed. They work anytime surgery is being performed, including emergency situations, so their hours can vary widely. Not surprisingly, their jobs can be quite stressful so stability, composure, and emotional control are all important traits. Computer knowledge is also important since they work with a variety of different software packages that are essential to their job performance.

Education and training

Education requirements for nurse anesthetists differ from other nurses because a bachelor's degree in nursing (BSN) is required before pursuing a master's degree (MSN) and the ultimate goal of a Certified Registered Nurse Anesthetist (CRNA). Aspiring nurse anesthetists can earn associates degrees, but the BSN is mandatory. In addition to required RN coursework, these students should expose themselves to psychology, physiology, surgery, mental health, sedation, anesthesia, Indi fluid therapy. This large amount of coursework is a lot to absorb, but it is necessary due to the job responsibilities and requirements of these professionals.

Nurse anesthesia master's degree programs are the next step for those who want to practice, but these programs require on the job experience, typically one year or more, before students are accepted. Courses are more specialized than those in the bachelor's degree program and typically consist of anesthesia-related pharmacology, biochemistry, and pathophysiology as well as surgery and pain management.

Once a master's degree is in hand, aspiring nurse anesthetists can take the National Certification Exam, which is typically required for the licensing necessary to become a CRNA and legally practice.

Practitioner nurse

Description

Practitioner nurses, commonly known as nurse practitioners, require more education, training, and certification than any of the other specializations discussed in this book because they have many of the same responsibilities as family practice physicians including prescribing medicine, performing physical examinations, and diagnosing medical conditions. In many states, nurse practitioners have the same authority as physicians and are not required to be supervised by them.

The role of nurse practitioners requires them to possess skills related to research, leadership, and analysis in addition to having practical knowledge and medical astuteness. They often have sub-specializations in areas such as oncology, pediatrics, mental health, and aging, and they find employment in public, private, or governmental settings.

In short, nurse practitioners are their own bosses because they make decisions regarding the health of their patients. They are independent leaders who have the knowledge, ability, and authority necessary to help people who are experiencing medical injuries or illnesses.

Education and training

Nurse practitioners must have a minimum of a master's degree in nursing order to practice; thereby requiring them to also possess a bachelor's degree. They also have to be licensed and certified; thereby making this specialization unique in terms of the amount of time and effort required to practice. Interestingly, there is a push by some people to require all nurse practitioners to earn a doctor of nursing practice degree (DPN) before they are allowed to become certified.

In the bachelor's program, aspiring nurse practitioners take the required RN classes in addition to courses on health, psychology, and physiology. Common courses in graduate programs include management, leadership, nursing theory, and human behavior.

After completing their master's degrees, aspiring nurse practitioners can work on becoming certified in their profession. This involves focusing on a sub-specialization as noted above and studying for and passing the required examination. Similar to operating room nurses, nurse practitioner certifications expire after a period of time and re-certification is necessary in order to maintain licenses.

Summary

Nurses are medical professionals whose value in health-care cannot be over-emphasized because they perform a wide variety of tasks in many different roles. They have changed the practice of medicine by diagnosing and treating patients as they see fit, which is something that only physicians could do in the past.

This book focuses on nurses. It examines the major specializations of these medical professionals including licensed practical nurses, registered nurses, pediatric nurses, oncology nurses, intensive care nurses, operating room nurses, nurse anesthetists, and nurse practitioners. Each specialization is described and the necessary education and training are discussed. The text is informational and educational, and it is written for easy understanding at all reader levels.

Congratulations! You now understand more about specialized nurses….professionals dedicated to the health and well-being of people all over the world.

Psychologists

Short and Simple Explanation Series
Book 6

Louis Bevoc

Published by
NutriNiche System LLC

Louis Bevoc books...simple explanations of complex subjects

Introduction

This is the sixth book in a series of short and simple explanations of professions. For every book, the profession is described along with a discussion on the required education and training. These books are written so people can inform and educate themselves on various professions without having to understand difficult language or complex terminology...which is the underlying philosophy of all Louis Bevoc books.

When people think of psychologists, they often think of therapists who treat people with mental problems who cannot help themselves. It is true that psychologists deal with troubled issues of the mind, but there is much more to these professionals than most people realize. They need to take into account the many factors that influence the way human beings behave such as have feelings, emotions, opinions, viewpoints, biases, and misunderstandings. These factors require a broad set of skills, some of which need to be discussed in this book to get a better understanding of the roles psychologists play in society.

Skills

Reading comprehension - Psychologists need to be strong in the area of reading comprehension so they can process and understand what they are reading. Without this skill, they miss information that could be important for solving problems and making life better for their patients

Writing - Psychologists need to understand the importance of their own writing because that writing must be understood by the people who read it. Psychologists' writing can be somewhat dry and boring, so it is imperative to keep it clear and concise to prevent readers from drifting off or not understanding the subject matter. In short, a strong grasp of the English language and the ability to put words into terms understood by the average person are important aspects of writing that needed by Psychologists.

Speaking - It is essential that psychologists have a strong grasp of the English language and the ability to communicate their message to those who lack familiarity with technical jargon. Without this skill, listeners will likely lose interest and not understand what is being said.

Listening - Psychologists need to ask questions for clarification, avoid finishing sentences, and prevent themselves from interrupting if they truly want to understand the key points others are making. Active listening is an acquired skill, and psychologists need to make that acquisition if they want to do their jobs properly. In short, psychologists must be able to listen actively to people or they will miss information that could be critical for their work.

Patience - Anyone who has conducted research is well aware of the fact that it requires time to complete. This time can be relatively long, and it requires patience in order to wait it out. Psychologists often find themselves in situations where they are required to wait in order to collect data, look for correlations, and make changes. For this reason, patience is a skill needed by psychologists in order to effectively do their jobs.

Social awareness - Part of social awareness involves emotional intelligence. Emotional intelligence is the capacity of someone to understand the feelings of others while controlling their own feelings. Psychologists who are emotionally intelligent understand people, listen to what they are saying, and react without becoming upset or distraught. They create harmony at work and make sound judgments.

Counseling - Counseling is, and should justifiably be, a necessary skill for professional psychologists before they are awarded a degree and authorized to practice in the field. After all, psychologists who are not capable of counseling others are not fulfilling one of their most basic duties. Quite simply, without counseling skills, a person should not have the title of "psychologist."

Self-sufficiency – Psychologists need to know how to manage themselves without direct supervision. They must understand what needs to be done and move forward with that understanding to accomplish goals and objectives.   In short, they must be capable of doing the things they need to do.

Quantitative research – This type of research is specific and numbers based. It investigates *who, what, when,* and *where* using statistics or mathematics. It uses manipulated variables and numerical data to establish findings that are used for improvement. An advantage of quantitative research is it provides precise numerical data that is not influenced by the researcher's personal bias, but a disadvantage is it produces numbers that are not specific enough for application in other situations.

Qualitative research – This type of research is much broader than quantitative research, using several different ways to gather data. It using uses interviews, focus groups, and observation to investigate *why* and *how* in addition to *who, what, when, and where*. An advantage of qualitative research is it can be used for complex studies, but a disadvantage is it can be influenced by the researcher's personal bias.

Critical thinking - Critical thinking skills are important for all psychologists because they need to accurately assess situations in order to make the best possible decisions. As critical thinkers, they need to identify problems, formulate approaches to those problems, and conduct research regarding those problems. After the research is conducted, they need to apply the findings in ways that benefit employees and organizations.

People unfamiliar with psychology programs are typically not aware that those programs offer two types of doctoral degrees. These degrees are known as PhD vs. PsyD, and they have differences and similarities. In terms of similarities, they both train students in the field of psychology so those students can become professional psychologists. However, differences between these degrees also exist as shown below.

PhD vs. PysD

PhD programs – PhD is an acronym for doctor of philosophy. These psychology programs are generally more accepted than PsyD programs. This acceptance is partially due to the focus being on academic research, but it also takes more time to complete PhD programs, they have been around longer, and they are more traditional than those offered for PsyD degrees.

The traditional status of PhD programs allows for more stipends and scholarships than those given for PsyD programs. They are also scientific research based, making them more acceptable in education. About three quarters of all doctoral degrees in psychology are PhDs.

PsyD programs – PsyD is an acronym of a doctor of psychology. These psychology programs have been offered for over a half-century, but they have not been around nearly as long as PhD programs. The PsyD is geared toward non-academic practice with a focus on clinical testing and various aspects of psychotherapy; thereby making it closer to that of an MD when compared to the PhD program.

PsyD programs are often easier to get accepted into than PhD programs, but they can also be harder to find the internships that often necessary for entering into practice. This is rather interesting considering PsyD students typically receive clinical experience faster and more frequently than students in PhD programs

The above explanations of PhD and PsyD programs are quite basic, but they eliminate some of the confusion that occurs when comparing these degrees. However, regardless of the differences involved, graduates of PhD and PsyD programs are both intensely trained in the subject matter; thereby preparing them for licensing in psychology upon graduation.

Another misunderstanding regarding psychologists is their confusion with psychiatrists. These two professionals perform similar job functions, but they are not the same as shown below.

Psychologists vs. psychiatrists

The methodologies used by psychologists and psychiatrists for research, diagnosis, and treatment differ in ways that make them seem somewhat opposite. This is due to the fact that psychiatrists are licensed physicians who use traditional medical thinking to diagnose and treat mental health problems. In short, they treat issues with medications rather than therapy or other non-medical interventions that alter perceptions and behavior. Psychologists, on the other hand, are not medical doctors and are generally not authorized to prescribe medications so they treat mental issues with medicine alternatives.

Psychiatrists and psychologists also differ in terms of education and training. Psychiatrists are highly educated and trained in medicine and they tend to use medical interventions to resolve mental health problems. Psychologists are educated and trained in psychological testing and analysis, and they typically solve mental health problems using counseling. This difference in education results in psychiatrists doing the majority of their training in medical facilities while psychologists primarily train in therapy-based clinics.

Interestingly, psychologists and psychiatrists sometimes refer their patients to each other. Psychiatrists refer their patients to psychologists when extensive psychological testing is required before decisions are made regarding the prescribing of medication. Conversely, psychologists refer their patients to psychiatrists when more expertise is needed in internal medicine or neurology.

There is much more about the similarities and differences between psychologists and psychiatrists that could be discussed, but that discussion is not necessary for this book. The main point to take away from this section is that psychologists treat health issues primarily by changing behavior while psychiatrists treat mental health issues primarily by prescribing medication. These two professionals have the same ultimate goals, but their methods of achieving those goals are different.

Now that you have a basic understanding of the roles psychologists play in the field of mental health, let's move forward to the next section that discusses the major types of these professionals. Please keep in mind that these types can be reduced in number, increased in number, or sub-categorized based on differing viewpoints and opinions. However, the goal of this book is to provide basic familiarity with the field of psychology rather than discuss the boundaries of its categorization.

Types

Types of psychologists and their job descriptions are listed below.

Clinical psychologist

Description

These specialists might be the most well-known type of psychologist due to the way the profession has been popularized in society. The general perception of "listening to people as they lie down on a sofa" fits them fairly well because they listen to people's problems and help them find solutions. However, it should not come as a surprise that this perception does not justify their existence. They treat people with mental and/or behavioral disorders, but the knowledge and skills necessary to do so require a wealth of education, training, and experience.

Specific disorders treated my clinical psychologists include depression, anxiety, emotional distress, substance abuse, and stress. Since they treat people of different ages, genders, cultures, religions, and races, they are sometimes sub-categorized into further specializations of people or conditions. Examples of further specializations of people include young children, adults, prisoners, celebrities, clergy, combat veterans, and BGLT. Examples of further specializations of conditions include stress, anger, schizophrenia, addictions, and phobias.

Clinical psychologists' work with their patients can be short-term or long term, depending on their diagnosis of those patients' needs. They work to treat causes instead of symptoms, and the determination of those causes takes varying amounts of time. Observations, tests, and discussions with patients and others are often necessary to find out what is needed for treatment and the prevention of reoccurrences.

Treatment is often therapeutic in order to get patients to analyze their situations, expose their feelings and emotions, and work on ways to alter their thought processes and change their behavior. If the need for medication is evident, then most clinical psychologists refer their patients to psychiatrists or other health care professionals who can prescribe the necessary medication.

Employment

Clinical psychologists work in many different types of healthcare settings including those found in hospitals, prisons, educational institutions, government agencies, and private practices. This wide range of employment opportunities is available because they diagnose and treat behavioral issues and disorders of the mind...problems that occur everywhere in society. Essentially, their specialization is applicable to the masses, which makes them unique when compared to other types of psychologists

Education and training

Clinical psychologists can get a PhD, but they typically obtain PsyD degrees based on their desire to practice outside of academic institutions. The focus of their education is clinical work, and it usually includes an internship where they receive practical experience that prepares them for work after graduation and passing of the required exams.

Child psychologist

Description

Child psychologists help children with mental and developmental issues. Specifically, they treat kid's problems such as depression, anger, anxiety, and other emotional issues. Their work involves assessment, diagnosis, and treatment, and most of that treatment focuses on therapy and counseling designed to help their patients develop new mindsets that lead to behavioral changes. If their therapeutic attempts are unsuccessful or they believe prescription medication is necessary, most child psychologists refer their patients to other health care professionals such as psychiatrists or psychiatric nurses.

Specific disorders treated by child psychologists include manic depression, obsessive-compulsive disorder (OCD), dyslexia, attention deficit syndrome, and mental issues brought about by tragedy or trauma. They need to develop working relationships with their patients and, because those patients are children, this requires skills that many other types of psychologists do not need. They often use drawings, pictures, figures, sporting events, dolls, or toys to put their patients at ease and get them to open up about their issues. Once the children open up, diagnoses can be made and treatment can be recommended.   Typically this treatment involves therapy or counseling designed to change thoughts and behaviors.

It is not uncommon for medical doctors to recommend their young patients to child psychologists for psychological analysis. The tests used by child psychologists are often the best way to determine social disorders, emotional issues, or learning disabilities. Diagnoses can yield specific information that addresses the individual needs of children who do not require prescribed medication.

Child psychologists are also different than other specialists in their field because must communicate with people other than their patients. They have to explain all assessments, diagnoses, and treatments to parents or legal guardians and, in some situations, school administrators. This communication requirement can add stress and complexity to their jobs, especially if the people they are educating are not familiar with child psychology processes and procedures.

Employment

Child psychologists often work in educational institutions, hospitals, or private practice. Those who work in private practice typically run their own businesses and are not bound by geographical areas or the types of mental issues children are experiencing. Those who are employed in educational institutions occupy positions as counselors or school psychologists. Last, but certainly not least, those who work in hospitals often treat children who have been traumatized or are experiencing more serious mental issues such as hallucinations or suicidal thoughts.

Education and training

Child psychologists typically complete a PhD or PsyD program that includes an internship. Their classroom work and real-world experience are needed to pass a required examination before they are certified to practice. Once in practice, they often undergo additional training to enhance their skills or focus on further specialized areas of their profession.

Criminal psychologist

Description

These specialists mostly focus on issues involving crime. They provide guidance for crime site investigators who are trying to find suspects. In this role, they do a lot of research in order to profile those who might have committed the crimes. Often times this entails reviewing old cases and establishing trends in personality traits, physical appearance, social skills, demographics, and other aspects of people's lives that might relate to criminal behavior.

Criminal psychologists are often thought of as the same as forensic psychologists. These two professionals have similarities because they both work on crime-related issues. However, their differences are as follows:

> *Criminal psychologists* – These psychologists focus on aspects of crimes before they have been solved, such as establishing criminal motives and determining criminal profiles, in order to determine why the crime was committed and who did it.

> *Forensic psychologists* – These psychologists focus on the aftermath of crimes, such as assessing the mental state of criminals and treating the damage those criminals have done, in order to establish justice and help victims.

Based on the similarities, it is understandable that people confuse criminal psychologists and forensic psychologists, but it needs to be mentioned that there is a distinct difference between them.

Since criminal psychologists do their jobs before crimes are solved, they work on assumptions and theories while attempting to help find the perpetrators who are involved. These assumptions and theories often come in the form of profiling where patterns and common traits define the type of suspect. For example, they might use information available from the crime scene or scenes (for serial crimes) to determine that the suspect is a young male who is a loner and has trouble maintaining relationships with others.

Employment

Criminal psychologists mostly work in private practices, police departments, or government agencies. They also teach courses at colleges and universities, as full-time faculty or adjunct professors, due to their extensive knowledge of law enforcement and suspect profiling. In police departments, they aid investigations by helping officers understand criminal minds. In government agencies, they often work to develop generalized profiles for specific types of crimes such as serial killings and white collar fraud.

Education

Criminal psychologists usually complete a PhD or PsyD program in general psychology that includes an internship. This internship often takes place at some type of law enforcement agency where the aspiring psychologists work with people who understand criminal profiling. Good places to gain this experience include the FBI, CIA and other government agencies that investigate criminal activity. Once they are practicing, criminal psychologists have opportunities to hone their skills by taking specialized courses in profiling, law enforcement, or rules and regulations within the legal system.

Industrial/organizational psychologist

Industrial/organizational (I/O) psychologists study workplace behavior by applying psychological principles and methods to organizations. Their ultimate goal is usually to get employees to perform at higher levels using motivational tools and strategies. Specifically, they work to improve employees' motivation and commitment to their organizations. Surveys are often used to tap into the feeling of workers, and the results indicate workplace improvements that need to be made.

I/O psychologists are very involved with change in workplaces. They work with employees to help them accept, and hopefully embrace, changes that take place in their organizations. In additional to using surveys that involve number crunching, these professionals also meet with individuals and groups to remove barriers to change; thereby making it easier for employees to accept that change.

I/O psychologists are different than other specialists in their field because they work strictly with employees. In this capacity, they hear about personal problems, but the focus of their job is to listen to employees about work-related issues that can be changed to improve productivity in organizations. In short, they believe that happy employees are more productive than unhappy employees...and many leaders agree with their thinking.

Employment

I/O psychologists are typically employed in private practice, companies, or academia where they apply their skills to workforces or teach them to students. In private practice and as employees of companies, I/O psychologists often focus on research using quantitative and qualitative methodology to gather information that can be used for improving productivity. However, they also move beyond research into leadership positions because they understand the needs of employees and motivate them based on that understanding. In academia, I/O psychologists typically teach their profession to students, but they can also be employed by schools as counselors or therapists.

Education

I/O psychologists typically earn a PhD or PsyD in psychology and then they obtain their license to practice. However, not all jurisdictions require these professionals to possess licenses. For example, some states do not require licensure for consulting roles (roles where they do not work directly for their client). Other states do not require a doctoral degree; thereby allowing I/O psychologists to practice with a master's degree. However, most companies only recognize certified I/O psychologists and those without that certification are not considered for I/O psychology positions.

Neuropsychologist

Description

Neuropsychologists study the relationship between people's behavior and their psychological processes. More specifically, they diagnose and treat neurological disorders by examining the functioning of the human brain. Many of their patients have experienced some type of brain damage that affects their behavior or cognitive skills.

Some people confuse neurology with neuropsychology, but they are actually quite different. Neurologists focus on the functioning of the nervous system while neuropsychologists focus on the functioning of the brain. Neurology is linked to physiology while neuropsychology s linked to cognitive psychology. Both professions study the human body, but neuropsychologists prescribe therapeutic treatment while neurologists prescribe medical treatment.

Neuropsychologists are very familiar with brain-based neurological tests such as magnetic resonance imaging (MRI) and computed tomography (CT). This familiarity is unique in the field of psychology because most psychologists diagnose patients after questioning or observation rather than after medical testing.

Employment

Neuropsychologists are typically employed in research facilities or research departments of organizations. Examples of potential employers include hospitals, research laboratories, rehab centers, medical clinics, prison systems, and government agencies. These professionals also have opportunities in law enforcement, but those jobs are usually reserved for forensic and criminal psychologists due to their specialized training. However, regardless of where they are employed, neuropsychologists diagnose and treat patients with neuropsychological disorders to change those patients' thoughts and behavior.

Education

Like many other types of psychology specialists, neuropsychologists need to obtain a PhD or PsyD. However, a BS degree in neuroscience rather than psychology is sometimes preferred for entrance into doctoral programs. Another differentiating aspect of education for neuropsychologists is the requirement of a post-doctoral fellowship before being allowed to obtain a license and practice. This requirement is difficult because post-doctoral fellowships are usually only given to the best students; thereby resulting in some people not being able to become licensed neuropsychologists.

Social psychologist

Description

Social psychologists study group processes and the environment that engulfs those processes. They often bridge the gap between sociology and psychology because sociologists study societal relationships and interaction while psychologists study individual human behavior. Social psychologists connect these two professions by studying the conditions that affect people's behavior and thoughts. In other words, they focus on situations that lead to people's behavior rather than the behavior itself.

Social psychologists diagnose and treat problems that have a broad ranging effect with the help of groups, organizations, or legal entities. Support comes in the form of money for research and the advancement of community awareness. An example is an organization that provides money to a group of university social psychologists who are working to prevent violence against women. The money is used to conduct research and create a marketing campaign that raises awareness of the problem and gets people to join in the fight against it

In some ways, social psychologists are similar to industrial/organizational psychologists because they work to improve systems as a whole. However, these two professionals differ because industrial/organizational psychologists limit their focus to workplace issues while social psychologists assess general problems in society. In short, social psychology encompasses a much broader range of issues that are in need of improvement.

Employment

Social psychologists sometimes work in private practices or as employees of organizations. However, they are more often found working in universities or government agencies due to the fact that their work is very research geared with long-term goals. Their studies can be quite costly because some never end. For example, finding new ways to assist poor people is something that continues on endlessly because there has always been, and will always be, poverty. Those who escape poverty are fortunate, but there are always those who cannot get out and new generations repeat the cycle.

Education

Social psychologists can find work with a master's degree, but many organizations and academic institutions will not employ them without a PhD or PsyD. However, regardless of the type of degree earned, aspiring social psychologists' course work must focus on statistics, study design, and research methodologies due to the fact that research will be prominent in their careers.

Interestingly, social psychologists usually do not have to be licensed in order to practice. The reason for this lack of requirement is not fully understood, but it has been said that it is because they treat societal issues rather than individuals; thereby reducing the risk that they will harm others based on diagnoses and treatments.

Health psychologist

Description

Health psychologists are unique in the field of psychology because they have more interaction with medical professionals than any of the other specialists due to their exploration of relationships between mental health and physical health. Their research uses linkages or connections found between mental and physical health to prevent health related problems in communities, populations, or society as a whole.

Similar to social psychologists, health psychologists' jobs are often research geared. However, they differ from social psychologists because they deal directly with individuals. For example, they conduct studies to find how people's immune systems are affected by their thoughts and behavior. They also explore genetics and their relationship to the mind.

Some health psychologists further specialize their research into focusing on particular diseases such as aids, cancer, or heart-related issues. They explore the relationship of people's minds and these diseases in order to prevent or reduce their occurrence. In this role, health psychologists tend to become experts in their field, and that expertise is sought by medical professionals.

Employment

Health psychologists tend to work in hospitals, medical clinics, rehab centers, universities, and government agencies. They focus on research and explore ways to prevent or irradiate diseases, often working on teams with specific agendas. Again, similar to social psychologists, health psychologists' research can be expensive and ongoing...but the results are worth the wait if health improvement breakthroughs are discovered.

Education

In order to practice in their field, health psychologists are required to have a PhD or PsyD in psychology. There degree program usually includes an internship and, in many cases, a post-doctoral program. This educational process is rather rigorous, but it does a good job preparing aspiring health psychologists for the real world problems that they will ultimately encounter.

Board certification is also mandatory in most states, and this mandate requires passing an examination given by a certifying board in health psychology. Many practicing health psychologists seek additional training or certification in specific areas in order to expose themselves to new methodologies and/or develop specialized skills.

Summary

Due to the continually increasing demand for mental health care, more and more psychologists are finding employment all over the world. As mental health care issues become more specific, so does the need for specialized psychologists who focus on particular areas of psychology in order to provide the best care possible. Specialization makes sense from a business and practical perspective, and it will likely continue well into the future.

This book is part of a series that provides short and simple explanations of different professions. It focuses on psychology specializations including clinical psychologists, child psychologists, criminal psychologists, industrial/organizational psychologists, neuropsychologists, social psychologists, and health psychologists. Each specialist is discussed in terms of job description, employment opportunities, and education necessary for practicing in academia or business. The text is informational and educational, and it is written for easy understanding at all reader levels.

Congratulations! You now understand more about psychology specialists....professionals who play a major role in the mental health care of people and society.

Writers

Short and Simple Explanation Series
Book 7

Louis Bevoc

Published by
NutriNiche System LLC

Louis Bevoc books...simple explanations of complex subjects

Introduction

This is the seventh book in a series of short and simple explanations of professions. For every book, the profession is described along with a discussion on the required education and training. These books are written so people can inform and educate themselves on various professions without having to understand difficult language or complex terminology...which is the underlying philosophy of all Louis Bevoc books.

Writers are people who communicate thoughts and idea through words. Sometimes these words are designed to be part of a process such as those composed by songwriters or playwrights, but the goal is always to communicate with others. Achievement of this goal can be hindered by misunderstanding, but the written word has survived the test of time and is still one of the most popular ways to communicate with others.

Writing is skill because everyone is not created equal in terms of expressing thoughts and ideas with words. Examples include newspaper columnists and novelists who are better at writing than others...especially if their readership is high. However, regardless of the number of people reading the work, some people stand out above others when putting their thoughts into words.

Writing is also an art because it allows people to express themselves. Writers of poetry are certainly artistic, as are movie scriptwriters and songwriters. These individuals put their thoughts into words to express their creativity in ways that others find enlightening, inspirational, or insightful. When people write artistically, they expose part of themselves that that might not be exposed when using other communicating mediums.

The biggest advantage, and sometimes disadvantage, of writing, is its permanence. For example, written contracts are binding by law and cannot be broken unless all parties involved agree to do so. This irreversible process is good for people who want the contract to remain as is, but it is bad for people seeking to change it.

This book focuses on several types of writers. It breaks each type into subcategories for better understanding while noting the differences that make them distinct. Please note that different types of writers and sub-categories of those types can be debated forever...and still there will be no definitive terms because people will always disagree. However, for simplification purposes, this book breaks down writers into basic types including creative writers, informational writers, performance writers, correspondence writers, and non-specific writers. Each type is broken down into subcategories that are described for easy understanding at all reader levels.

Now that you understand the focus of this book, let's move forward to discussing specific types of writers. Please note that certain writers fall into more than one type. For example, (1) a playwright could be considered a creative writer, (2) a newspaper reporter could be considered an informational writer, and (3) and educational reference writer could be considered technical writer. All of these considerations cannot be addressed in a book of this magnitude, so the writers were put in the categories deemed best by the author.

Creative writer

Creative writing is a subject offered in most high schools and colleges. Students are assigned the task of putting their thoughts and ideas on paper by inventing characters, giving opinions, discussing current events, or writing about anything else where they can freely express themselves without the fear of being inaccurate or wrong. The goal of these assignments is to get students' "creative juices" flowing about something they find passionate or interesting.

The following are specific types of creative writers:

Poet

Poets are one of the oldest type of creative writers because they have existed in some form since words were first written. They express their thoughts and ideas by literally, metaphorically, symbolically, or figuratively writing about something, and their work is intended to be read by others for inspiration, pleasure, or other emotional stimulation.

True poets understand rhyming words are not necessary for their work. In fact, some poets rarely ever write pieces that rhyme because they prefer to do otherwise. They consider themselves to be creative writers, and creativity tends to elude them if their words are forced to rhyme.

Songwriter

In many ways, these professionals are poets who take their writing to the next level by turning words into lyrics that are inserted in songs. These lyrics are designed to provoke emotional responses from readers, but those emotional responses are often dependent on the accompanying music. Also similar to poetry, song lyrics do not have to rhyme…although many people expect them to do so because they help the song "flow" and make the words easier to remember.

Songwriters are unique writers because people often remember every word that they have written for a particular piece of work. When people like songs, they tend to learn all of the words so they can sing along with those songs. Poems can also be recited from memory, but the addition of music makes it even easier to remember the words in songs.

Novelist

As indicated by their name, novelists are writers who create something new using words. They typically write a story with characters and a plot that appeals to specific genres of people. For example, a love story attracts readers who might not be interested in a novel based on a football team.

Novelists need a great deal of creativity because they write thousands of words in their stories. They need to keep their readers' attention by providing interesting stories that flow smoothly, make sense, and are captivating. Their stories are more detailed than shorter pieces written by other creative authors, and that is why novels sometimes take years to finish.

Short story

These writers often create mini-versions of novels. Their stories have characters and plots, but they are much shorter than novels. In fact, some short stories are only a few thousand words. However, regardless of the length, short stories require creativity on the part of their authors and that is why they fall under the creative writer type.

Short story writers are unique because they must be able to share a story with a limited amount of words. This might appear easy to do because less has to be thought about and written. However, a short story can actually be more difficult to write than a novel because authors need to know what information needs to be included in their stories in order to make them flow smoothly and entertain their readers.

Advertising and marketing

The writers influence people to purchase products and services. They do this by using catch phrases, play-on-words, and similar wording that plays on the emotions of the people they are trying to entice. They must be talented because they need to write persuasive messages using very few words due to reasons including cost, loss of attention, and information overload. In the world of written advertising and marketing, every word counts and "less often means more" in terms of sales dollars generated.

Copywriters are often employed as creative writers in advertising agencies and marketing firms. Many people are familiar with the job title of copywriter, but they confuse "copyright" with "copywrite" and assume copywriters work on legally protecting written work and intellectual property...which is simply not true. Copywriters have nothing to do with legal proceedings or the law in general. Rather than providing brand protection, they work to promote brand awareness. They create copy for billboards, newspapers, brochures, commercials, social media, and other advertising material in order to drive the brand awareness necessary to increase sales.

Advertising and marketing writers are unique because they gear their work toward specific audiences. The research their targeted market in advance and gear their words specifically for the people in that market. For example, an online advertiser for a Boston Bruins hockey jersey might target 20 to 30-year-old, single, white males with annual incomes of $40,000 or more. The wording of the ad mirrors normal language commonly used by these individuals; thereby providing them with a level of comfort that entices them to buy the jersey.

In terms of education, there are no formal requirements for creative writers. However, college level courses in English, grammar, composition, and creative writing are certainly helpful. Readers who find grammar mistakes, spelling mistakes, weak writing, or confusing dialog are likely going to stop reading the creative piece and move on to something else.

Informational writer

These writers provide information on topics that are typically fact-based. They write about people, places, events, and things that provide knowledge about the subject matter. Examples include writing about famous people, historical sites in Europe, the impact of immigration, or new technological breakthroughs in medicine. Regardless of the subject being discussed, informational writers provide fact-based information for their readers.

The following are specific types of Informational writers:

Non-fiction

These writers provide information for readers who want to learn about the subject matter. Examples include autobiographies, biographies, vacation destinations, business endeavors, organizational descriptions, historical landmarks, and many other topics that interest readers and are not fiction-based. The credibility of non-fiction authors usually stems from their experience with the topic; thereby making them authoritative figures whose writing is trustworthy and believable.

Writers of non-fiction convey information that is not a fantasy or made up so some people assume that all non-fiction writing is based on facts. However, this assumption is not entirely accurate.   Non-fiction work depicts reality, but it is not necessarily fact-based. For example, a plant manager who writes a plant management reference book is writing based on his experiences and memory. However, there are no documented facts that his memory or experiences are factual. Readers simply believe what he writes because he appears to be an experienced plant manager who understands his job well and has established himself as an authority on the subject matter.

Reference

Reference writers are authors of works such as dictionaries, encyclopedias, and other books that provide information. These references help readers understand the subject matter so they can solve problems, finish projects, write papers, or do just about anything else that requires knowledge of the information found within the pages of the book.

Reference books are unique because they are rarely read "cover-to-cover." Instead, people refer to them for specific reasons such as the spelling of a word or meaning of a phrase. Rarely will people state they enjoyed a reference book because the information within is typically for practical or education-based purposes rather than pleasure.

Interestingly, some reference writers fall into other categories including technical manual writers and academic writers. Examples include writing style books such as those designed to teach people the American Psychological Association (APA) and Modern Language Association (MLA) rules and regulations. These books are thought of as manuals for writing in a particular style, but they are also used as references, and they are almost exclusively used by students in educational institutions.

Manual

These professionals are similar to reference writers, but they tend to focus on more specific audiences. For example, a refrigerator manual typically only pertains to the people who own the refrigerator in that manual while a dictionary pertains to many different people including those who own refrigerators.

Manuals are not written for entertainment purposes and are often considered "dry" reading. However, they serve an important purpose because they document processes and procedures that make people's lives easier, less expensive, and more convenient. Manuals impact virtually everyone in one way or another and, without them, people would encounter problems that are challenging to resolve.

Academic

Academic writers provide research, reviews, and overviews of particular topics in education. They typically write papers, reports, articles, chapters in books, or books (usually textbooks). Their work is usually geared toward a specific audience and is sometimes only understood by that audience. For example, a textbook chapter on the qualitative methodology used by industrial/organizational psychologists might use terminology that might only be understood by readers with a background in psychology.

Academic writers overlap with other types of writers, but they deserve to be mentioned as a specific category because their work is closely monitored for style, structure, and content. This monitoring is unlike any other monitoring because it is quite intense, and deviation from established rules and protocols can cause authors' work to become flawed or invalid.   For example, academic researchers who write journal articles must follow specific protocols for submitting those articles or their work will not be published.

There are no formal requirements for non-fiction writers, but they should have experience in the subject matter for credibility purposes. Reference writers usually have some type of college background, but their education also has no formal requirements and their experience in the subject matter is often considered more important. Academic writers, however, typically have advanced degrees at the college level. Their degrees offer credibility that they understand the subject matter based on their formal education and training.

Performance writer

Performance writers specialize in writing words that are spoken by others who are attempting to entertain, influence, or motivate their audiences. The speakers of their words can be actors, actresses, comedians, entertainers, politicians, business people, and other people who speak to audiences using scripted material. Their words can be spoken live, such as a political speech given by a gubernatorial candidate, or they can be recorded and presented at a later date or time, such a line spoken by movie actor.

The following are specific types of performance writers:

Play

Many people find plays enjoyable, and the individuals who write those plays are commonly known as playwrights. Playwrights write dialog for actors who perform on stages for audiences that range from a few people to several thousand people. Their work is typically theme based with characters involved in specific circumstances.

Playwrights must put a great deal of thought into their work because their words must fit the characters and themes involved in order to be well received by audiences. Additionally, plays take place in restricted workspaces with limited props. Scenes are able to change, but not to the extent that they can be changed in television or film, so the audience must be able to visualize what is happening based on the dialog. These factors make it challenging to write plays that will hold the audiences' attention from beginning to end.

An interesting note about playwrights is that they are also scriptwriters because they write scripts for plays. However, while all playwrights are scriptwriters, all scriptwriters are not playwrights.

Speech

Speeches are one of the most effective ways to reach large audiences, and people who write those speeches are commonly known as speechwriters. They specialize in writing the words that others say to audiences. Although some speeches are recorded, most are given live for a more convincing or dramatic effect….especially if they are intended to be motivating such as a sales seminar or a victory celebration.

Speechwriters need to choose their words carefully to get their messages across and avoid offending people in their audiences. This is not a simple task because audience members can be quite different from each other…especially if the speech applies to a demographically diverse group such as a political speech that affects a large population of people.

Speechwriters are most likely to find employment with politicians who need to give many different speeches. However, these professionals also work for people who speak at funeral homes, wedding celebrations, groundbreaking ceremonies, honorary banquets, reunions, and educational functions.

Script

Scripts provide dialog for many different types of performances, and people who write those scripts are commonly known as scriptwriters. Scriptwriters write for television, radio, movies, musicals, and other forms of entertainment that require dialog.

Scriptwriters need to understand their audiences in order to invoke desired reactions to the dialog. For example, horror films typically attract different audiences than situation comedies, so the same dialog usually does not apply. However, regardless of the type of audience, scripts need to follow a theme or the connection with that audience will not be made.

Performance writers do not require a formal education, but most have been in college classrooms and many have college degrees. Education is important because it exposes these writers to various situations that require the use of their skills. Unlike other writing professionals, college coursework provides real-world experiences for performance writers because they can find local audiences with relative ease. In fact, many colleges have their own radio and/or television stations that can be used to "test the waters" and obtain immediate feedback.

Correspondence writer

These types of writers correspond with others on a professional level. They often are a direct link to the public, and, depending on their popularity, their work can be read by millions of people.

Correspondence writers are often thought of as documenting facts, even though some of their work is based on personal beliefs. Without these professionals, people all over the world would not get the information they need to make choices and form options.

The following are specific types of correspondence writers:

Reporter

Reporters, also known as journalists, provide written information and insight on topics of interest. They perform research, conduct interviews, gather data, and inject their own thoughts into their work; thereby providing a detailed analysis of the subject matter for their readers.

These professionals typically work for newspapers, magazines, and various other print and online sources. Some reporters skim the top of the topic they are writing about while others dig deep to provide a much more investigative report. However, regardless of the depth of their coverage, reporters provide written correspondence for their readers.

Reporters are unique among writers because their jobs have evolved to include a wide variety of ethical standards. They are supposed to be objective in their approach; thereby allowing their readers to form viewpoints based on facts rather than beliefs or opinions. However, as might be expected, unbiased reporting is often not the norm. In fact, some reporters focus strictly on bias writing such as those who work for liberal or conservative news organizations that are known for only supporting one side of the story.

Editor

These individuals are technically considered correspondence writers, but most of their writing involves correcting the written work of others. Essentially, editors act as reviewers of documents to make those documents read well and fit into particular areas of newspapers, magazines, websites, etc.

Editors hold a wealth of power in organizations that publish written words. This power is over the writers of these words, and many times those writers are angry or resentful over having their work critiqued and/or altered. They feel like their creativity is being stifled or suppressed, especially if their editors make substantial changes deemed necessary to improve flow, structure, or readability.

Most editors understand their responsibilities and do their best to make sure changes are only made when necessary. They are experienced professionals who know how to improve their writers' work. However, there are editors who make unnecessary alterations to the documents they review, and these individuals can cause a log of unwarranted grief and aggravation.

Critic

Most people are familiar with the saying, "everyone is a critic." Unfortunately, this is true in many situations. However, true critics do more than criticize; they also point out positive aspects and offer suggestions for improvement. For writers, pointing out positive aspects works as a motivational tool for progress. Without some type of "pat on the back," writers become discouraged...and some stop writing altogether.

High-profile critics have many followers. Readers of their work wait to see what they have to say about writing pieces before they begin to read them. This might seem bias and unfair, but, unfortunately, it occurs on a regular basis. Critics are powerful correspondence writers, and their opinions are valuable to a lot of people.

In addition to being understanding and insightful, critics must be good writers if they are going to attack the written work of others. Critics with poor writing skills are not taken seriously by their readers...and, ironically, their work might end up being the target of other people's criticism.

Documentarian

These writers document something that has happened or is currently happening. Documentarians tell stories using facts, figures, data, and other supporting information. These writers need to be careful not to present the supporting information in a biased manner if they want their audiences to form opinions and make informed decisions.

Documentarians who focus solely on written words are becoming more and more a thing of the past. Their decreasing presence is due to the fact that people find radio and film documentaries more entertaining due to the paralanguage, non-verbal communication, and visual effects that add to the stories. However, regardless of their popularity, these writers deserve mention because they are a variable aspect of the correspondence category.

It is not uncommon for correspondence writers to be college educated. In fact, some employers require a college degree in journalism or something similar before a person is considered for a writing position. These professionals hone their writing skills and research techniques in the classroom and then move into real-world jobs in some type of reporting or journalistic capacity.

Non-specific writer

These writers do not fall into any of the other categories discussed in this book, so they make up a category of their own. Non-specific writers sometimes write professionally, but they more often choose to compose for themselves or specific others including family and friends. Based on this choice, they often write informally for more intimate communication, and they trust the people who read their work.

The following are specific types of non-specific writers:

Letter writer

Email and text messages are currently the most popular methods of written communication that have, for all practical purposes, replaced much of the letter writing that took place in the past. However, letters are still used today because they add personal or professional touches to the messages being sent.

Letters can be very private, such as a love letter, or very public, such as a letter for a public offering of stock. However, regardless of their intended secrecy, letters relay a message from senders to receivers...and those messages are often very important. For example, a letter from an attorney about a lawsuit has financial importance, and a letter from a friend discussing the death of a loved one has emotional importance.

Personal letter writers are unique because they are not bound by rules regarding substance or subject matter. They can write about almost anything of interest to themselves or the people on the receiving end. The same message can be sent in electronic form, but a handwritten letter provides a much more personalized form of communication.

Ghostwriter

People who write for others and let those others take credit for their work are commonly known as ghostwriters. This is a fairly common practice and, aside from some ethical concerns, is acceptable for many different types of writing including stories, autobiographies, song lyrics, newspaper columns, and magazine articles.

Ghostwriters typically do not expose themselves as the authors of their written work. In fact, they often sign an agreement that requires them to remain silent. This silence has benefits because, if the ghostwriters are good, they usually get referrals for work on other projects. However, the lack of credit can also prevent them from stabling themselves as well-known authors to the people who read their work...which makes them truly unique among non-specific writers.

Diarist

Diaries help people reflect back on their thoughts and actions to get a snapshot of where they were and how they felt at a particular point in their lives. This reflection can evoke a wide variety of emotional responses that segregate this type of writing to a different category than any other written material.

Diaries are likely the most unique type of non-specific writing because they are very personal and are often never intended to be read by anyone other than the author. Many diary writers go to great lengths to protect their work, but they are often unsuccessful. People look at what the diarists have written without their approval or knowledge and they form opinions or draw conclusions that might or might not be accurate. In fact, diaries have been used for historical purposes to piece together what the world was like at certain periods of time. An example is the diary of Anne Frank. Anne's work shed light on her personal situation and gave people an insight into the German military occupation during World War II.

People who write diaries should always remember that, regardless of the preventative measures implemented, their work might be read by people other than themselves. This means diary writing involves risk that must be taken seriously by writers who chose to document their behavior and the behavior of others.

Non-specific writers do not require any formal education. However, ghostwriters should have taken some English and/or creative writing coursework at the college level because they are writing for others. Grammatical and spelling errors are almost always deemed unacceptable by the people who are using ghostwriters' work, as are stories that do not flow properly, follow a theme, or make sense to the reader.

Summary

Writing is a concept that has been around for centuries. It tells stories, provides entertainment, relays history, documents actions, and provides a wealth of information about unlimited topics. It has many different rules and regulations depending on where it takes place and who oversees it, but it always serves as a form of communication between people.

This is the seventh book in a series of short and simple explanations of professions. It focuses on specific types of writers including creative writers, informational writers, performance writers, correspondence writers, and non-specific writers. These writers are broken down into subcategories and the need for each is defined and discussed. The text is informational educational, and it is written for easy understanding at all reader levels.

Congratulations! You now understand more about writers….people who use their skills to influence others all over the world.